Globalization and the Erosion of National Financial Systems

NEW DIRECTIONS IN MODERN ECONOMICS
General Editor: Malcolm C. Sawyer,
Professor of Economics, University of Leeds, UK

New Directions in Modern Economics presents a challenge to orthodox economic thinking. It focuses on new ideas emanating from radical traditions including post-Keynesian, Kaleckian, neo-Ricardian and Marxian. The books in the series do not adhere rigidly to any single school of thought but attempt to present a positive alternative to the conventional wisdom.

A list of published titles in this series is printed at the end of this volume.

Globalization and the Erosion of National Financial Systems

Is Declining Autonomy Inevitable?

Marc Schaberg

University of California, Riverside

NEW DIRECTIONS IN MODERN ECONOMICS

Edward Elgar

Cheltenham, UK • Northampton, MA, USA

Published by
Edward Elgar Publishing Limited
Glensanda House
Montpellier Parade
Cheltenham
Glos GL50 1UA
UK

Edward Elgar Publishing, Inc.
136 West Street
Suite 202
Northampton
Massachusetts 01060
USA

A catalogue record for this book
is available from the British Library

Library of Congress Cataloguing in Publication Data
Schaberg, Marc. 1970–
    Globalization and the erosion of national financial systems : is declining autonomy inevitable? / Marc Schaberg.
    (New directions in modern economics series)
    Includes bibliographical references and index.
    1. Finance. 2. Monetary policy. I. Title. II. Series.
HG173.S264 1999
332.4—dc21   99–15586
                                                        CIP

ISBN 1 84064 159 2

Printed and bound in the United Kingdom at the University Press, Cambridge

Contents

Tables		*vii*
Figures		*ix*
Introduction		*xi*

1.	Financial Systems	1
	Financial Systems	1
	Comparing Financial Systems	7
	Significance of Financial System Differences	11
2.	The Structure of Financial Systems	15
	Decomposing Uses: Investment and Financial Asset Purchases	15
	Other Dimensions of Financial Systems	19
	Long-Term Patterns of Financing	20
	US	24
	UK	27
	Japan	31
	Germany	35
	France	39
	Conclusion	43
	Appendix	45
3.	Financial Systems and Investment	48
	Introduction	48
	The Standard Two-Price Model	49
	Borrower's and Lender's Risk and Financial Structure	50
4.	External and Internal Finance	63
	Appendix	75
5.	Investment, Financial Asset Purchases and Sources of Funds	78
	The Composition of Investment Financing	78
	Financial Asset Purchases: Precautionary and Speculative	81
	The Volatility of Investment	83
	Investment and Sources of Funds	84
	Internal Finance and Investment	98
	Conclusion	100
	Appendix	103
6.	Globalization and the Convergence of National Financial Systems	105
	Globalization of Financial Markets	105

Quantity Measures of Integration   107
Price Measures of Integration   108
Is the Present Period of Financial Market Integration
Historically Unique?   110
Globalization and the Convergence of National Financial
Systems   111
Convergence   112
Conclusion   132
Appendix   135
7. Policies for the New Financial Environment   137
Introduction   137
Policy Implications of Results on Globalization and
Convergence   141
Dismantling Direct Controls and Credit Allocation
Mechanisms   146
Policies for the New Financial Environment   149
Conclusion   156
References   159
Index   175

Tables

2.1   Investment and stock and bond purchases as shares of gross
      sources of funds: 1970–1995   16
2.2   Net sources of finance: 1970–1994   20
2.3   Gross sources of finance: 1970–1994   22
2.4   Uses of funds: 1970–1994   23
2.5   Net sources of finance: US   26
2.6   Uses of funds: US   27
2.7   Net sources of finance: UK   29
2.8   Uses of funds: UK   30
2.9   Net sources of finance: Japan   33
2.10 Uses of funds: Japan   34
2.11 Net sources of finance: Germany   37
2.12 Uses of funds: Germany   38
2.13 Net sources of finance: France   41
2.14 Uses of funds: France   42
A2.1 Gross sources of finance: US   45
A2.2 Gross sources of finance: UK   46
A2.3 Gross sources of finance: Japan   46
A2.4 Gross sources of finance: Germany   47
A2.5 Gross sources of finance: France   47
4.1   Volatility of bank finance: 1970–1994   64
4.2   Volatility of internal funds: 1970–1994   64
4.3   Cash flow – bank finance correlations: 1970–1994   65
4.4   Volatility of ready funds: 1970–1994   72
A4.1 Gross bank finance – cash flow regressions   75
A4.2 Regression of gross bank finance on cash flow, output, and
      investment   76
5.1   Investment as a share of output: 1970–1994   80
5.2   Investment as a share of total gross sources: 1970–1994   80
5.3   Investment volatility: 1970–1994   84
5.4   Regressions of investment on total gross sources of funds 90
5.5   Regressions of investment on ready funds: 1970–1994   97
A5.1 Investment – cash flow regressions: 1970–1994   103
A5.2 Regressions of investment on cash flow and output   104

6.1 Time trend regressions – standard deviations of net and gross internal and bank finance for the five countries: 1970–1995   114

6.2 Internal funds deviations – trend regressions: 1970–1995   121

6.3 Bank finance deviations – trend regressions: 1970–1995   125

6.4 Standard deviations of investment – adjusted uses of funds ratios: trend regressions 1972–1995   129

6.5 Standard deviations of stock and bond purchases – adjusted uses of funds ratios: trend regressions 1972–1995   132

A6.1 Time trend regressions – bank finance: 1970–1995   135

A6.2 Time trend regressions – internal funds: 1970–1995   136

Figures

2.1	Investment as a share of total gross sources	17
2.2	Stock and bond purchases as a share of total gross sources	18
2.3	Net sources of finance – US	25
2.4	Net sources of finance – UK	28
2.5	Net sources of finance – Japan	32
2.6	Net sources of finance – Germany	36
2.7	Net sources of finance – France	40
3.1	The standard two – price model	50
3.2	Borrower's risk and ties to lender	54
3.3	Borrower's and lender's risk in the two systems	56
3.4	A reduction of cash flow in an exit-dominated system	57
3.5	A reduction in cash flow in a voice-dominated system	57
3.6	The impact of different levels of borrower's risk	59
4.1	First differences of gross bank finance and internal finance – US	66
4.2	First differences of gross bank finance and internal finance – UK	67
4.3	First differences of gross bank finance and internal finance – Germany	68
4.4	First differences of gross bank finance and internal finance – France	69
4.5	First differences of gross bank finance and internal finance – Japan	70
5.1	Investment as a share of output	79
5.2	Investment and total real gross sources – US	85
5.3	Investment and total real gross sources – UK	86
5.4	Investment and total real gross sources – Germany	87
5.5	Investment and total real gross sources – France	88
5.6	Investment and total real gross sources – Japan	89
5.7	Investment and ready funds – US	92
5.8	Investment and ready funds – UK	93
5.9	Investment and ready funds – Germany	94
5.10	Investment and ready funds – France	95
5.11	Investment and ready funds – Japan	96
6.1	Net internal funds deviations from exit model trend – France	118

6.2	Net internal funds deviations from exit model trend – Japan	119
6.3	Net internal funds deviations from exit model trend – Germany	120
6.4	Net bank finance deviations from exit model trend – France	122
6.5	Net bank finance deviations from exit model trend – Japan	123
6.6	Net bank finance deviations from exit model trend – Germany	124
6.7	Investment as a share of adjusted uses	127
6.8	Standard deviation of investment shares	128
6.9	Stock and bond purchases as a share of adjusted uses	130
6.10	Standard deviation of stock and bond purchases as a share of adjusted uses	131

Introduction

A growing literature has focused on the financial systems of various countries. The body of work concerns itself with the way countries finance investment and investigates the institutional arrangements different countries possess for channelling finance for investment projects. This book contributes to this literature.

The book empirically examines the patterns of sources and uses of funds in the non-financial enterprise sectors of the US, UK, France, Japan, and Germany. While there have been empirical comparisons on the sources of finance, there has been no work on the uses side. This book addresses how the uses of finance vary across these five countries and finds significant differences in the uses of funds patterns across financial systems. The book also provides recent data on the sources of financing for these countries. These data on sources of finance as well as the new data on uses allow an examination of an important question found in the literature on financial systems. The question is whether the structures of the financial systems in these countries have converged as financial market globalization has proceeded. This question is addressed empirically by examining time series of sources and uses of funds and by performing econometric tests for convergence on these time series.

The possible effects on investment of the differing institutional arrangements countries have for financing that investment are also examined. This examination is conducted by empirically comparing the patterns of uses of funds, which include investment, across financial systems. The book further explores the relationship between investment and financial systems. It examines the possibility that differences in financial systems produce different relationships between flows of financing and investment at the macro-level. This possibility is approached through a model of investment developed by Minsky (1975). The model is adapted to take into consideration the possibility that the institutional arrangements for financing investment will have an impact on the relationship between the behaviour of internal finance, external finance and investment.

The question of whether complete convergence and declining policy autonomy are inevitable is then addressed. The book examines how the changes in financial markets and financial systems considered in the book have impacted on monetary and financial policy. The book further explores the convergence of financial systems by examining the convergence in the conduct of monetary policy in the US, UK, France, Japan, and Germany and the removal of credit allocation policies in several of these countries. In light of the evidence on changes in financial systems, the book proposes policy measures designed to deal with these changes in a way that promotes productive investment and limits financial speculation.

The structure of the book is as follows. In Chapter 1, an overview of the literature on financial systems is presented. This chapter also discusses some of the measurement issues involved in comparing financial systems.

Chapter 2 of the book empirically examines the patterns of sources and uses of funds in the non-financial enterprise sectors of the US, UK, France, Japan, and Germany. This chapter also addresses how the uses of finance vary across these five countries and finds that significant differences in the uses of funds patterns exist across financial systems. Recent data on the sources of financing for these countries are provided. These data lay the foundation for examining an important question found in the literature on financial systems: have the structures of the financial systems in these countries converged as financial market globalization has proceeded?

Chapter 3 explores the possibility that differences in financial systems produce different relationships between flows of financing and investment at the macro-level. There has been much firm-level work on the relationship between cash flow and investment as well as macroeconomic research on the relationships between cash flow, credit flows, and investment.[1] However, there has been almost no research on how these relationships might vary across financial systems. This book addresses these potential variations. Adapting a model of investment developed by Minsky (1975) suggests that the relationships between internal finance, external finance, and investment might vary across financial systems. The model is adapted to take into consideration the fact that the institutional arrangements for financing investment will have an impact on borrower's and lender's risk and therefore on the relationships between and behaviour of internal finance, external finance, and investment.

Chapters 4 and 5 then explore empirically if in fact these relationships differ across financial systems. Chapter 4 focuses on the relationship between external and internal finance while Chapter 5 investigates the relationship between investment, financial asset purchases and sources of funds. This empirical work provides new insight into the differences among financial systems.

Chapter 6 empirically addresses the question of whether or not the financial systems discussed in the book have converged by examining time series of sources and uses of funds and performing econometric tests for convergence on these time series.

The final chapter further explores the convergence of financial systems by examining the convergence in the conduct of monetary and financial policy and the removal of credit allocation policies in countries with voice-dominated financial systems. The chapter examines the policy implications of this convergence based on the empirical evidence presented in the book. The chapter then proposes policy measures designed to deal with the emerging problem of declining autonomy associated with globalization and convergence of financial systems.

NOTE

1 Empirical work on the relationship between cash flow and investment includes, among others, Mott (1982), Fazzari and Mott (1986), Fazzari, Hubbard, and Petersen (1988), Fazzari and Athey (1987), and Fazzari (1993). On the macroeconomic relationship between cash flow, credit flows, and investment in the US, see Friedman and Kuttner (1993), Calomoris, Himmelberg and Wachtel (1995), and Perry and Schultze (1993).

1. Financial Systems

FINANCIAL SYSTEMS

A review of the literature on financial systems helps to place some of the specific contributions of this book in context. The literature on national financial systems is an outgrowth of a much wider body of writings having to do with the relationship between finance and industry. This broad collection of work includes Marx (1981) and his discussion of the relationship between money capitalists and industrial capitalists. Hilferding (1910) builds on this work and examines how banks become important suppliers of credit to industrial firms. He argues that bank credit increasingly consists of long-term financing of investment projects, giving the banks growing interest in the long-run health of industrial borrowers. Here, Hilferding develops his notion of 'finance capital' defined as 'capital at the disposition of the banks which is used by the industrialists' (Hilferding, p. 226).[1] Schumpeter (1912) is also concerned with the relationship between banks, as providers of credit, and industrial firms as this relationship relates to economic development.

With this broader body of work on the relationship between finance and industry as prologue, the literature pertaining to differences in national financial systems begins with Gerschenkron (1962).[2] He examines European industrialization from the mid-nineteenth century to World War I and puts forward three different patterns of financing across countries. For Gerschenkron, the type of financing pattern observed in a country is tied to the level of development and the timing of its initial industrialization. Short-term bank lending dominated external financing in England due to the early and gradual industrialization that occurred there. Because of this pace and timing of development, business people had sufficient capital accumulated and were not forced to rely on long-term external funds. In Germany, however, with the industrialization process occurring later and more rapidly than in England, firms required larger amounts of external capital. Banks developed relationships with firms to which they provided both long-term financing and managerial assistance. Gerschenkron notes how Germany served as a model for the 'universal banks' found in other European countries. The third pattern of financing Gerschenkron discusses is that of Russia. He argues that countries like Russia that were undeveloped and possessed little national wealth and a scant history of business institutions would not be able to develop a banking sector with sufficient capital to finance industrialization. These countries thus required the government to direct financing for investment by discouraging consumption through taxation. With this classification of financial systems and the comparative nature of his analysis, Gerschenkron inaugurates the literature on how countries' institutional financial arrangements relate to their financing of investment.

The literature continues with Carrington and Edwards (1979). They are concerned with the amount of long-term financing being directed toward real investment in various countries. Carrington and Edwards see real capital investment in a country as partially a function of its financial systems. They investigate the financial systems of France, Germany, Japan, the UK and the US. They criticize the US and UK financial systems as featuring what they call the 'Anglo-Saxon' tradition of financing. This tradition is one in which banks shy away from making long-term loans to firms with high debt levels, most investment is financed out of profit retentions, and the stock market is a small source of new financing (Carrington and Edwards, p. 190). Carrington and Edwards argue that these practices limit firms' ability to invest and grow. In France, Germany, and Japan they find a high degree of integration of banking and industry where firms have higher debt to equity ratios and that bank loans are a major source of investment finance. In these countries with bank-based financial systems, Carrington and Edwards argue, firms are able to secure a much higher degree of external long-term financing for investment than their counterparts in countries with capital market-based financial systems.[3]

Zysman (1983) builds on the binary categorization of countries' financial systems into bank-based or capital market-based offered by Gerschenkron and Carrington and Edwards by developing a third dimension focused on the extent of government involvement in these systems. He examines the same countries as Carrington and Edwards and classifies them into three groups based on three criteria. First, like Carrington and Edwards and Gerschenkron, Zysman is concerned with the way a country transforms savings into investment and envisions two possibilities. In what he calls 'credit-based' financial systems, the transformation is made through banks or other institutions taking deposits and then extending loans to firms. In 'capital market-based' systems, investment funds are obtained by issuing securities sold in markets (1983, pp. 63-4). The second dimension Zysman then considers is how prices are set in these loan and securities markets. The possibilities here are competitive prices, institution-dominated prices, or government-fixed prices (1983, p. 69). The third dimension consists of the roles played by governments in the financial system. Zysman categorizes governments by whether they give priority to controlling monetary aggregates or to allocating credit between competing uses and whether they pursue these ends administratively or through market incentives.

Taken together, these three dimensions define three different types of financial systems. The typology consists of first, capital market-based systems where security issues are the dominant source of long-term industrial financing, the central bank primarily concerns itself with controlling monetary aggregates, and prices are largely competitive. Zysman argues that Britain and the United States fit this capital market-based model. The second type of financial system is a credit-based system with government-administered prices. Here banks provide critical long-term financing and the government sets prices in some markets to allocate financing. France and Japan are Zysman's examples of this second model. Credit-based systems with institution-dominated prices constitute the third type of financial system. This third type differs from the second in that here the state pursues aggregate goals through market operations instead of allocative goals through administrative action. Zysman argues that Germany is a prime example of this third type of financial system.

Zysman's addition of the third dimension of government's role in the financial system is instrumental to his purpose of examining the institutional context within which governments pursuing industrial policy can be effective as well as the response of countries to industrial change. He finds significant differences among countries based on their type of financial systems, their adjustments to industrial change and the efficacy of each government's industrial policy. Specifically, the government's ability to use selective credit allocation policies determines whether or not there can be an effective industrial strategy.

Like Zysman, Rybczynski (1984, 1985) is interested in the implications of different financing patterns on countries' industrial growth. He claims there are two basic types of financial systems: 'bank-oriented systems' and 'market-oriented systems'.[4] Rybczynski's categorizations are consistent with the binary distinction between the bank-based and market-based systems of Gerschenkron and Carrington and Edwards. These two types are seen as stages in the evolution of the financial system in the course of economic development. Bank-oriented systems are marked by heavy dependence of firms on finance largely in the form of loans from financial intermediaries. Market-oriented systems are characterized, in his schema, by firms' dependence on capital markets to obtain financing in the form of marketable securities – both equity and debt (1984, p.278). Rybczynski argues that the financial system of a country will progress through these stages from a bank-oriented system to a strongly market-oriented system. As a country moves through these stages, he claims it is improving the risk-bearing capacity of the economy and thereby increasing capital formation, savings, and economic growth (Rybczynski 1985). Risk is central to Rybczynski's understanding of financial systems and their evolution. He views the financial system 'as an arrangement for bearing and allocating risk' (1985, p.38). Rybczynski argues that the market-oriented system of the UK performs well in this function (1985, p.35).

Berglöf (1990) approaches the question of financial structure from the vantage point of incomplete contracting theory, where firms' debt contracts do not and cannot fully specify the required actions for every possible state of nature. He follows the work of Zysman and Rybczynski with respect to the distinction between 'bank-oriented' and 'market-oriented' systems. He defines the industrial finance system as 'the institutional arrangements designed to transform savings into investments and to allocate funds among alternative uses within the industrial sector' (1990, p.243). He examines six countries, adding Sweden to the list of countries examined by Zysman. Berglöf finds two fundamentally different financial systems and terms them bank-oriented and market-oriented (1990, p.257). He argues that the incomplete contracting literature could interpret these differences in financial structure as showing differences in the allocation of risk and control across investors and states of nature. Berglöf focuses on the lack of restrictions on commercial banks in bank-based systems that allows them to hold both debt and equity of firms. He argues that this allows banks to exercise control more effectively and makes them willing to extend credit beyond levels seen in market-oriented systems. He argues that this in turn allows for more internal conflict resolution in distressed firms, helps solve the principal - agent problem between debt and equity holders and creates more stable ownership structures.

Frankel and Montgomery (1991) also take issue with the standard classification of some of the advanced economies' financial systems. They examine the financial structure of the US, UK, Germany and Japan with the focus on comparative levels of bank performance in those countries. Their interests and emphasis thus differ from those who have approached the area of comparative financial structures with an interest in assessing the role of financial structure in financing real investment and spurring economic growth. Frankel and Montgomery find that the frequent characterizations of the German and Japanese systems as bank-oriented systems and the United States as a market-oriented system are supported by their investigation

(1991, pp.266-8). However, they reject the common conception of the UK as a market-oriented system like the US by showing that banks have dominated the provision of external financing, as in Germany and Japan.[5]

In another study of the financing patterns found in the advanced economies, Borio (1990) investigates the differences in the leverage and financing of non-financial companies in the G-7. He uses flow of funds data to calculate different measures of leverage in these countries. Borio finds that, using data through the mid-1980s, the traditional distinction between low-leverage countries (US, UK, Canada) and high-leverage countries (Germany, Japan, France, Italy) still provides a useful classification. However, he also finds that these differences began to narrow from the early to mid-1980s due in large part to the heavy merger and leveraged buyout activity that increased the level of leverage in the US.

Jacobs (1994) provides a statistical examination of the validity of the common division of various national financial systems into their respective categories. He performs a cluster analysis of twelve countries' financial systems based on data from the 1970s and finds empirical justification for the more common binary division of national financial systems into bank-based and market-based systems as well as Zysman's tripartite division discussed above.[6]

Grabel (1997) provides an in depth description of the financial systems of the US, UK, Germany, Japan, and South Korea. She terms these systems 'national financial complexes'. Grabel argues that a country's financial complex influences the level and composition of a nation's investment portfolio. She gives detailed descriptions of the attributes of these five national financial complexes and discusses some of the stylized differences in investment in these countries.

Mayer (1987, 1988, 1990, 1994) explores the connection between financial systems and investment further in a series of articles. Like Berglöf, he is interested in how theories of incomplete contracting relate to the financial structure; that is, how observed patterns of finance can be viewed with respect to the issue of control. Mayer uses a slightly different approach to taking measure of a country's financial structure. Mayer uses flow rather than stock data and all financing proportions are on a net basis.[7] To calculate these proportions on a net basis, acquisitions of financial assets are subtracted from increases in corresponding liabilities (1990, p.329). On the basis of these financing proportions, Mayer compares the financing patterns of eight countries: Canada, Finland, France, Germany, Italy, Japan, the UK, and the US. Mayer parts with the standard classifications of financial systems as either bank-based or market-based systems and instead makes several unique observations. Among them, Mayer observes that retained earnings are the dominant source of finance in all countries, in no country do firms raise a substantial amount of finance from securities, and in all countries banks are the dominant source of external finance (1990, pp. 310-7). Mayer goes on to argue that control theory can explain these financing patterns, in particular why banks provide a majority of external finance across countries. In this work, Mayer takes issue with the characteristic division of developed economies into bank-based systems and market-based systems.

In later writing Mayer (1994) distanced himself further from this characteristic division and developed his own typology of economies based on two classes of economies: 'banking economies' and 'market economies'. This division is based on differing relationships between corporate ownership patterns and the structure of financial systems. He argues that banking economies have small proportions of companies quoted on stock exchanges, high concentration of ownership and long-term relations between banks and industry. Market economies display high proportions of quoted companies, low concentrations of ownership and short-term relations between banks and industry (1994, p. 9). Mayer argues for his typology by claiming that there are not any significant differences in the 'structure or behaviour of Japanese and German banks from those in the UK or US' (1994, pp. 8-9). The important difference, according to Mayer, is between the capital markets of these countries. He then discusses the concentration of ownership and the number of listed companies in these four countries and argues the US and the UK are market economies and Germany and Japan are banking economies.

Other authors who have worked with the framework developed by Mayer include Edwards and Fischer (1994), Bertero (1994), and Corbett and Jenkinson (1996).[8] This strand of the literature on financial systems is important for this book because it attempts to measure patterns of financing based on flow of funds data, which is one of the methods that will be employed here.

Edwards and Fischer (1994) reject attempts to characterize the UK and German systems as either bank-based or market-based systems. They present measures of financing sources for the UK and Germany. Edwards and Fischer claim that Germany should not be regarded as a bank-based system nor is the UK a market-based system because Germany does not rely on bank loans to a greater extent than the UK and internal funds comprise the largest source of funds in both systems.

Bertero (1994) examines the French financial system. She too measures the pattern of financing sources by using flow of funds data. Bertero discusses the deregulation of the French financial system and how this has impacted on the pattern of financing up to 1991.

Corbett and Jenkinson (1996) construct a comparative set of data on the sources of finance for investment for the UK, US, Germany, and Japan and, like Edwards and Fischer (1994) and Mayer (1990) before them, challenge some of the conventional views about international differences. They conclude that there is no 'market-based' pattern of financing in the US and UK. These systems are more properly understood, they argue, as internally financed with small or negative contributions from market sources.

Pollin (1995) uses the 'exit/voice' framework of Hirschmann (1970) to describe the differences between the two types of systems. In this framework, holders of securities exercising influence by selling their securities, that is, by utilizing their 'exit' option, characterize the Anglo-Saxon, capital market-based systems. In contrast, voice-dominated financial systems are characterized by, among other attributes, closer ties between banks and industrial firms, with banks providing a higher degree of long-term financing and less well-developed secondary markets for financial assets. In these systems, influence is exercised by using 'voice' with institutions, both public and private, actively involved in shaping the long-term plans of firms and committed for a longer time period. One of the reasons these differences in financial systems are significant is because the structure of voice-dominated systems allows for a long-term view regarding investment as opposed to the short-term bias of exit-dominated systems (Pollin, 1995).

This book contributes to the literature on financial systems by providing measurements of patterns of financing sources for the US, UK, Germany, Japan, and France from 1970 to 1994. It provides the most recent measurements of these patterns and provides five more years of data than the most recent work on the issue by Corbett and Jenkinson (1996). The book also contributes by making adjustments to the data on the US that improves international comparability. In addition, the book brings a new perspective to the discussion of financial system differences by focusing on how the patterns of uses of funds differ across exit-dominated and voice-dominated financial systems. The literature on financial systems has focused on the sources of financing without explicitly considering the uses of these funds and how these uses may differ across countries with varying financial systems.

COMPARING FINANCIAL SYSTEMS

In this book's comparison of financial systems, the main emphasis is on comparing how the non-financial corporate sectors of each country finance investment. The patterns of financing of both physical investment and total investment by non-financial corporate enterprises in different countries are compared. As will be discussed, there are several measurement questions and problems to be addressed in undertaking this kind of comparison. For example, differences in corporate governance structures and other institutional differences might not be captured by measurements of financing patterns but may impact on the cost of capital or the behaviour of investment.

Company Accounting Data vs. Flow of Funds Data

Comparing capital gearing or leverage ratios of non-financial businesses in different countries allows the comparison of financial structures in different countries. This type of comparison is usually performed using stocks of liabilities and assets from company accounting data. These kinds of comparisons have several measurement problems that have to do with differences in accounting practices and the sources of the data. International differences in accounting practices produce balance sheets that are not exactly comparable. For example, there are international differences with respect to whether assets are reported at book value or are revalued periodically with market prices. In Japan and Germany revaluations are legally forbidden and all assets are valued at historic cost while in the UK and the US revaluations are allowed, albeit more uncommon in the case of the US (Corbett and Jenkinson 1994). Furthermore, book values of assets and reserves are sensitive to depreciation schedules and accounting practices regarding depreciation vary across countries. The source of the data for leverage ratio comparisons also presents a problem.[9] Comparisons of capital gearing ratios are usually made from data on aggregate company accounts. These types of accounts, including the *OECD Financial Statistics Part 3*, are only available for particular samples of firms that are not necessarily representative of the non-financial corporate sector as a whole.

These and other problems with international comparisons based on balance sheet data have led to arguments in favor of using flow of funds data (Mayer 1990, Edwards and Fischer 1994, Corbett and Jenkinson 1994). By using flow of funds data, one can see the source of funds in a particular year and the uses to which those funds were put. By using sources and uses information, one can then better answer the question of how the flow of investment was financed.

Measuring for Convergence

In this book, time series of sources of financing are calculated for five countries: the US, UK, France, Germany, and Japan. This allows an investigation of the question of the convergence of these financial systems. A comparison of the patterns of financing sources and uses of funds for these countries highlights whether the non-financial enterprises in these countries are becoming more similar. This book will answer the question of whether the voice-dominated systems of Japan, Germany, and France have become, by these measures, more like the exit-dominated systems of the US and UK.

Data Sources and Methodology

The sources of financing are calculated from flow of funds statistics and are reported both in time series of annual values and weighted five-year averages. For the US, the data come from the *Federal Reserve Board Flow of Funds Accounts Table F.102* and the *Federal Reserve Bulletin Table 1.46*. For the UK the *Office of National Statistics Financial Statistics Table 10.6B* was used. The *National Accounts Table for Account 1-Non-Financial Incorporated Enterprises* published by the Economic Planning Agency was used for Japan. For Germany and France *the OECD Financial Statistics Part 2, Financial Accounts of OECD Countries Tables 33F/01* and *33F/08*, respectively, were used. Original national sources were used for the UK and Japan because the data reported for these countries by the OECD is not strictly comparable to that reported by the OECD for France and Germany. The Federal Reserve Board data was used for the US because it is reported in greater detail and allowed for the exclusion of the farming sector, which the OECD includes in its US data. All of the data are flow of funds data for the non-financial enterprise sector. However, there are some slight variations across countries in the exact sectoral definitions. These are referred to in the individual country sections later in the chapter.

An accounting identity exists for flow of funds data so that in every period total sources of funds are equal to total uses of funds:

$$\text{TOTAL SOURCES} = \text{TOTAL USES} \qquad (1.1)$$

Disaggregating the total sources and uses so that each type of financing source is indexed by i and each use of financing is indexed by j yields:

$$\Sigma^I_{i=1} S_i = \Sigma^J_{j=1} u_j \qquad (1.2)$$

The financing of investment can be illuminated by flow of funds data in two ways. The gross sources of finance are calculated by finding the share of each type of finance in the total gross sources. Total gross sources of finance include internal funds measured as retained earnings before depreciation and the gross amount of increases in liabilities from bank loans, bonds, shares, trade credit, and other sources. The share of internal funds in total gross sources, for example is calculated by dividing the gross flow of internal funds by the total gross sources:

$$S_{internal} / \Sigma^I_{i=1} S_i \qquad (1.3)$$

The same calculation is done for each gross source of financing. Net sources of finance can be calculated by subtracting firms' acquisition of financial assets from the corresponding increase in liabilities. Total net sources of finance are equal to physical investment. This is evident from examining the accounting identity in equation 1.2 again only this time separating out physical investment (PI) from the total uses of funds.

$$S_1 + S_2 ... + S_I = u_1 + u_2 ... + u_3 + PI \qquad (1.4)$$

To calculate the total net sources each source of financing is subtracted from its corresponding use. For example equity purchases as a use of funds would be subtracted from equity issues as a source of funds and bank deposits as a use of funds would be subtracted from bank loans as a source of funds.[10] Thus, total net sources of funds is expressed:

$$TNS = (S_1 - u_1) + (S_2 - u_2) ... + (S_I - u_I) = PI \qquad (1.5)$$

This net measure helps answer the question of how the physical investment of the firm was financed by netting out the sources of funds used to buy financial assets. The share of any net source in total net sources is calculated by dividing that net source by total net sources. For example, equity as a share of total net sources would be found by dividing the net flow of equity--which is the gross flow of equity issues as a liability minus the gross purchases of equity as a financial asset--by the total net sources of funds:

$$(S_{equity} - u_{equity}) / TNS \qquad (1.6)$$

Both measures are useful for providing a measurement of a country's financial system, and together they provide information about financing patterns that either measure alone would fail to yield.

Weighted Averaging

The averages over time are found by calculating a particular source's share of total sources of finance for a whole period of time over that same period once all sources are converted to constant prices. This method of averaging sources of finance follows Mayer (1990), Corbett and Jenkinson (1994), Bertero (1994), and Edwards and Fischer (1994), although differences exist in the specific price indices chosen to convert sources to constant prices. Each average is weighted by the contribution of that source to total gross or total net sources by the value of the total net or total gross sources. This method of averaging has the advantage of avoiding giving equal weight to years in which little financing was raised and years in which a great deal of financing was raised. The weighted average for any period is computed as follows:

$$\Sigma^{T}_{t=k} (i^{j}_{t} * P_{t}/P_{1987}) / \Sigma^{T}_{t=k} (I_{t} * P_{t}/P_{1987}) \tag{1.7}$$

where i^{j}_{t} is the amount of financing source of type j in year t in the current price of year t, I_{t} is the sum of all types of sources, and P_{t} is the GDP deflator for year t.

SIGNIFICANCE OF FINANCIAL SYSTEM DIFFERENCES

Why do these differences in national financial systems matter? The literature on these systems goes beyond classifying the financial systems of certain countries to explore the relative merits of the different types of systems. A central question of this book is what are the effects of these differing institutional arrangements on the financing of investment in each of the countries in question. While the conclusion is not universal, a broad range of researchers has found the bank-based, or voice-dominated, systems to be superior to the capital market-based systems along a number of different dimensions.

First, voice-dominated financial systems better solve information, co-ordination, and incentive problems. One strand of this literature explores the principal – agent problem between owners and managers of firms and argues that bank-based systems do a better job of resolving this incentive compatibility than do capital-market based systems (Cable 1985, Berglöf 1989).[11] This superiority arises from the ability of banks in these systems to utilize close monitoring to gather better information than that available to widely dispersed investors. Thus, through devoted monitoring, banks with close ties to firms are better able to mitigate the information asymmetries between managers and owners than more dispersed owners because of the public good nature of monitoring (Stiglitz 1992a)[12]. Similarly, banks avoid the co-ordination problem that would plague a larger group of dispersed investors. Under these theories, close relations between banks and industry should yield higher firm performance. Empirically, Cable (1985) found a positive relationship between the degree of bank involvement in German industrial companies and their financial performance.

Another principal – agent problem addressed in this literature is that between shareholders and debtholders. The problem here is that a firm's shareholders have incentives to appropriate wealth from its debtholders by encouraging sub-optimal investments that run contrary to debtholders interests. Debtholders, aware of this problem, will require a higher interest payment from firms likely to have this problem. This will result in a lower optimal debt/equity ratio than would obtain in the absence of this agency cost. One way, in theory, to resolve this agency problem would be to have the debt and equity held by the same agent. In Japan, where banks are allowed to hold both debt and equity of firms, the agency problem is mitigated to a greater degree than it is in the US where banks are not allowed to hold both debt and equity. (Prowse 1990)

One additional common reason offered for the superiority of bank-based systems is their fostering of long-term time horizons and promotion of long-term productive investment. In those countries with bank-based financial systems, firms are able to secure a much higher degree of external long-term financing for investment. This compares with the 'short-termism' associated with capital market-based systems. Poterba and Summers (1992) found that US CEOs feel their time horizons are shorter than CEOs in Europe and Japan. They attribute this difference to the US equity market's undervaluing of long-term investment projects. A class of long-term investment projects that is undervalued by US capital markets is investments in 'high performance' work environments (Applebaum and Berg 1995). They argue that short-term financial market pressures make longer-term investments in people and workplace transformations that don't yield quick measurable returns extremely difficult to undertake. The financial markets in the US are thus seen as a constraint on long-term business strategy. They are also said to impact on managerial goals. For example, US managers rank return on investment and higher stock prices as their top two objectives while their Japanese counterparts rank improving product quality and introducing new products and increasing market share as their top two goals (Porter 1992).

Differences in financial structure also account for some of the differences in the cost of capital. Various studies have found the cost of capital during the 1970s and 1980s to be higher in the US than in Japan and Germany. The tighter integration of industry and finance in Germany and Japan is claimed to have allowed for higher leverage ratios without increasing bankruptcy risks to the same degree as well as lower direct costs associated with industrial firms' bouts of financial distress (McCauley and Zimmer 1989).

NOTES

1 Larry Neal (1990), in his economic history of the rise of financial markets in eighteenth-century Western Europe, develops the term 'financial capitalism'. 'Financial capitalism' is the phenomenon of financial markets directing the outcome of goods and factors markets (p.4).

2 Others, such as Cameron (1967), Goldsmith (1969), and Gurley and Shaw (1955) were early contributors to the role of the financial system in the development process. However, these authors do not compare financial systems or construct a typology as Gerschenkron does. Since it is this comparative aspect as well as the classification that is of interest here, these works, while important, will not be addressed here.

3 Carrington and Edwards point out that these bank-based financial systems generate funds for investment and not consumption. They contrast the level of credit received by consumers for both consumption and housing in these countries to the relatively greater amount seen in the US and UK (pp. 152-3).

4 Rybczynski also describes 'strongly market-oriented systems' which are market-oriented systems that have developed advanced risk-hedging (e.g. futures, options) markets and where financial institutions increasingly trade in their assets (securitization). However, the binary division of systems is consistent with his schema because his third category is concerned with the degree of market development and keeps intact the distinction between bank-based systems and market-based systems.

5 Frankel and Montgomery use flow of funds data on the net external funding of nonfinancial businesses for the four countries. They give averages over five year intervals for the percentage of business financing that come from the domestic securities markets and from domestic banks. On this basis they find that the UK raises more funds through bank loans, like Germany and Japan, while the US is more heavily reliant on securities, which are negligible in the UK.

6 Others who have contributed to the literature on financial systems are Cox(1986), Cumming and Sweet (1988), Porter (1992), and Goldstein (1995).

7 Mayer also gives gross financing measures but focuses his analysis on the net figures.

8 All of these authors, including Mayer, participated in the Centre for Economic Policy Research project, An International Study of the Financing of Industry.

9 Borio (1990) avoids the sampling problem of using company accounts by constructing gearing measures from National Income Accounts.

10 This is not to imply that there is a barrier to fungibility. The gross funds raised are clearly fungible. The funds raised from equity issues could be used to make bank deposits and funds from bank loans could be used to purchase equity. However, the fact that these funds are fungible does not invalidate the netting procedure. The net contribution of equities to the sector is still the gross issue of equity by the sector minus the gross purchase of equity by the sector.

11 A seminal work on financial/ownership structure as it relates to different agency problems, including both those between shareholders and debtholders as well as owners and managers, is Jensen and Meckling (1976).

12   Corbett (1990), writing about incentive incompatibilities and information asymmetries associated with the financing of industry, states 'one reason why banks may be better able to finance industry in these circumstances than arms'-length markets is that a long-term relationship with an element of confidentiality may provide a framework for an exchange of information which is otherwise difficult' (p. 211). This is consistent with Stiglitz's (1992a) assertion that 'in general, in markets with imperfect information and incomplete contracting, long-term relationships often enhance economic efficiency'(p. 22).

2. The Structure of Financial Systems

DECOMPOSING USES:
INVESTMENT AND FINANCIAL ASSET PURCHASES

The literature on financial systems has focused on the sources of financing to differentiate the types of systems (Borio 1990, Mayer 1990, Corbett and Jenkinson 1994, Bertero 1994, Edwards and Fischer 1994). I argue here that, in addition to differences in sources, significant differences exist in the uses of funds across financial system types. Specifically, exit-dominated financial systems invest a smaller share of total sources of funds and purchase a larger amount of financial assets as a share of total sources than do countries with voice-dominated financial systems. This is an important distinguishing characteristic of these financial systems that has not previously been explored. Not only does this measure serve to differentiate the two types of financial systems, but it also may inform the link between financial systems and investment. This idea will be explored in Chapter 3 of the book.

The propensity to purchase financial assets and to invest out of total sources of funds can be seen by decomposing the uses of funds into two types: physical investment and financial asset purchases and then calculating the ratios of each of these to total uses (sources). Recall equation 1.4 that had on the right-hand side the sum of all of the uses of funds indexed by j to represent their type. We can regroup these uses into three aggregates: physical investment (*PI*), stock and bond purchases (*SBP*), and other uses (*OU*):

$$\Sigma^I_{i=1} s_i = \Sigma^J_{j=1} u_j = PI + SBP + OU \qquad (2.1)$$

As a measure of the extent to which firms use their funds to finance physical investment, the ratio of investment to total sources is calculated as follows:

$$PI / \Sigma^I_{i=1} s_i \qquad (2.2)$$

A measure of the degree to which firms purchase financial assets out of total sources (uses) can be calculated as the ratio of stock and bond purchases to total sources (uses):

$$SBP/\Sigma^I_{i=1}s_i \qquad\qquad (2.3)$$

These two measures help differentiate voice-dominated financial systems from exit-dominated financial systems.

A characteristic of the exit-dominated financial system is that the non-financial business sectors of these economies purchase large amounts of financial assets out of their gross sources of funds or, put another way, they invest less of their gross sources of funds in real physical assets. Figure 2.1 shows a plot of a three-year moving average of physical investment as a share of total gross sources of funds for each country. The US and the UK invest less out of their total sources of funds than do Japan, France, and Germany. Figure 2.2 shows the three-year moving average of the ratio of stock and bond purchases to total gross sources. Germany, France, and Japan purchase fewer financial assets than the US or UK.

The averages of these investment and financial asset purchase shares along with their standard deviations over the whole period from 1970 to 1994 are given in Table 2.1.

Table 2.1: Investment and stock and bond purchases as shares of gross sources of funds: 1970–1995

Country	PI/TGS	σ	SBP/TGS	σ
Germany	78.6 per	0.072	4.3 per	0.024
Japan	70.1 per	0.171	1.8 per	0.015
France	65.2 per	0.107	9.0 per	0.073
US	54.4 per	0.092	9.3 per	0.052
UK	49.5 per	0.090	12.2 per	0.037

Source: Own calculations from *Federal Reserve Board Flow of Funds Accounts Table F.102.* and *Federal Reserve Bulletin Table 1.46* for the US, *OECD Financial Statistics* for Germany and France, *Economic Planning Agency National Accounts* for Japan, *and Office of National Statistics Financial Statistics* for the UK.

These figures demonstrate a clear ranking of the countries with respect to their investment out of gross sources of funds. Germany displays both the highest and most stable investment share of 78.6 per cent of total gross sources. Japan invests the second highest portion of total gross sources of funds at a level of 70.1 per cent although it displays the greatest variability.

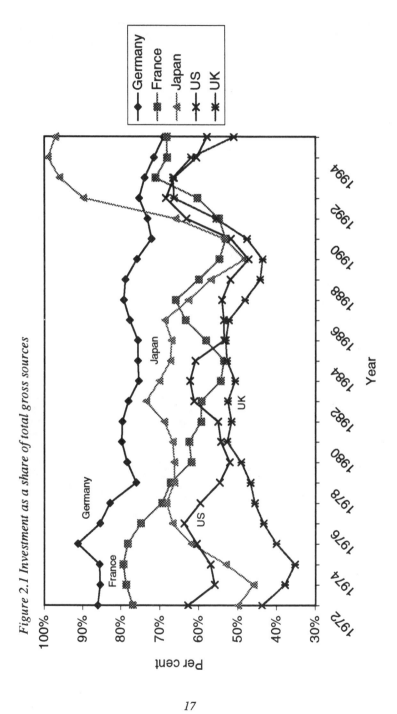

Figure 2.1 Investment as a share of total gross sources

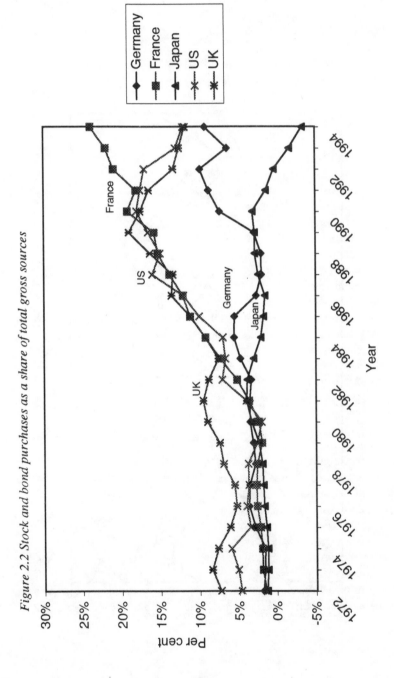

Figure 2.2 Stock and bond purchases as a share of total gross sources

France follows with 65.1 per cent of total gross sources going to physical investment. The exit-dominated financial systems of the US and UK invest only 54.4 per cent and 49.5 per cent of total gross sources. These exit systems invest considerably less of their funds than do the voice-dominated financial systems. Further analysis of the patterns of uses of funds over time across the countries in question is presented throughout this chapter.

OTHER DIMENSIONS OF FINANCIAL SYSTEMS

The pattern of financing is not the only important dimension of a country's financial system that can be observed by examining net and gross financing and decomposing uses of funds. Other dimensions include the institutional detail regarding the relationships between financial institutions and non-financial firms as well as the corporate ownership and governance structure. These institutional differences may help explain variations in financing costs, patterns of financing, and, as will be discussed in Chapter 3, investment and other macroeconomic behaviour.

Significant differences in institutional arrangements could be missed if one relies solely on data on the changing pattern of financing. Bertero (1994) examines the liberalization of financial markets in France with the specific aim of addressing the convergence thesis. The appearance of more marketable instruments, the increasing use of retentions and the reduction in the use of bank lending to finance investment shows convergence towards the pattern of capital market-based systems. However, Bertero argues that this story is incomplete because as these changes have not marginalized the banks but have instead enabled the new French universal banks to become 'the most important agents in the financial markets and, therefore, to remain the core of the French financial economy'(Bertero, 1994 p. 69). Entities called banks may remain central to the French financial system. However, if they lend to firms at a level that is a fraction of what they had lent in the past and firms significantly alter their pattern of funding sources and their use of these funds then, I argue, something fundamental has changed in the financial system. This chapter focuses, in part, on measuring these changes. While the entirety of a financial system should not be reduced to measurements of patterns of financing sources and how these funds are used, these measures provide a very good framework for understanding the structure of a financial system and how that structure may or may not be changing over time.

LONG-TERM PATTERNS OF FINANCING

Sources of Funds

Before detailing the changing patterns of financing for non-financial enterprises in the five countries under consideration here, long-term averages of net sources of finance are given. The first pattern that appears when examining the long-term averages of net financing sources in Table 2.2 is the heavy reliance on internal finance in the US and UK. In the US and UK 92.4 and 90.0 per cent respectively of physical investment is financed by retained earning. These figures are considerably higher than the corresponding 74.8 per cent for Germany, 72.1 per cent in France, and 65.3 per cent in Japan.

Table 2.2: Net sources of finance: 1970–1994

Source	US	UK	Germany	France	Japan
Internal	92.4%	90.0%	73.9%	72.1%	65.3%
Bank Finance	11.2%	13.7%	13.2%	16.0%	28.5%
Bonds	15.4%	5.2%	0.5%	4.8%	8.1%
Equity	–6.4%	–4.1%	-0.1%	4.5%	3.5%
Trade Credit	–5.0%	-0.5%	-0.9%	-0.6%	–4.8%
Capital Transfer	–	2.5%	8.7%	3.2%	–
Other	0.2%	3.4%	4.5%*	–	–0.1%
Discrepancy	–7.9%	–10.2%	0.0%	0.0%	0.0%

Notes: Provisions for pensions are what comprise this category for Germany. See discussion on pension provisions in the section on Germany below.

Source: Own calculations from *Federal Reserve Board Flow of Funds Accounts Table F.102*. for the US, *OECD Financial Statistics* for Germany and France, *Economic Planning Agency National Accounts* for Japan, and *Office of National Statistics Financial Statistics* for the UK.

Here we can clearly see two groups, the US and the UK, that are heavily dependent on internal sources of finance and Germany, France, and Japan that are not. The same groupings do not hold up as clearly, however, when bank finance is considered. The fact that Germany financed only 13.2 per cent of physical investment from bank sources while the UK financed 13.7 per cent makes problematic the comparison of Germany as a 'bank-based' system and the UK as a 'market-based' system. The relative weakness of bank finance as a source of funds in Germany, the fact that equity is a net drain on finance in the supposed market-based systems of the US and the

UK and the fact that equity is a net source of funds in France, Japan, and Germany further calls into question the taxonomy of market-based systems vs. bank-based systems. Mayer (1990, 1994) and Corbett and Jenkinson (1994) have challenged this market/bank characterization based on the weakness of 'market' sources of funds in the supposedly market-based systems of the US and UK and the relatively weak funding from bank sources in the supposedly bank-based German system.

Yet differences across the countries do exist at the net level and, in addition to other distinguishing characteristics of national financial systems discussed, on a purely quantitative level, two groups emerge. However, the groupings are not based on how much bank finance or market finance the non-financial business sectors receive but on the extent to which they are dependent on internal funds. The exit-dominated systems of the US and UK are heavily reliant upon internal funds while the voice-dominated systems of Germany, France, and Japan are not as dependent on internal funds as a net source of funds.

The gross sources of finance for the five countries over the period 1970 to 1994 are listed in Table 2.3. France and Japan are distinguishable from the US and UK on the basis of their uses of internal sources of funds. Internal funds in France comprise 45.5 per cent of gross sources and internal funds in Japan constitute 45.2 per cent of gross sources while the figures for the US and the UK are 57.0 per cent and 60.0 per cent, respectively. Germany, unlike France and Japan, relies on internal finance to the same degree as the exit-dominated systems of the US and UK. When gross bank finance is considered, the distinction between the exit-dominated systems and the bank-based systems becomes clear. The UK and US rely on bank finance to a considerably lesser extent than France, Germany, and Japan.

Previously, authors have been wary of making comparisons based on gross data involving the US (Corbett and Jenkinson 1994). This was largely because the data on equity given in the Flow of Funds Accounts is already a net figure. I have estimated both the gross issuance of equity and the gross purchase of equity by the non-financial corporate sector.[1] This makes possible comparisons based on gross sources data. When bond and equity sources of finance are considered together as 'market' sources of finance, then a clear distinction emerges between the two groups with one exception. The US and the UK have higher market sources of finance than the voice-dominated systems with the exception of France. The US relied upon bonds and equities for 18.1 per cent of its total gross sources of finance. The UK figure is 12.6 per cent while in Germany market sources accounted for 5.7 per cent of gross sources. These same sources accounted for 8.9 per cent of gross funds in Japan and 16.8 per cent in France. Two things need to be considered regarding the French figure for equity. First, this long-term average masks the extraordinary amount of change over time in France's pattern of financing as discussed later in the section on France. Second, the equity figures for France are not exactly comparable to those of the other countries because the equity category in France includes sources as equity that are not included in other countries (Bertero 1994). This overstates the amount of equity financing in France when compared to the other countries in question.

Table 2.3: Gross sources of finance: 1970–1994

Source	US	UK	Germany	France	Japan
Internal	52.4%	60.0%	56.9%	45.5%	45.2%
Bank Finance	8.5%	18.8%	26.3%	22.3%	32.0%
Bonds	9.9%	3.1%	2.3%	3.9%	5.7%
Equity	8.2%[a]	9.5%	2.4%	12.9%	3.2%
Trade Credit	6.6%	1.9%[b]	1.6%	13.3%	11.2%
Capital Transfer	–	1.7%	6.7%	2.0%	–
Other	14.4%	5.1%	3.5%[c]	–%	2.7%

Notes:
a. The Flow of Funds Accounts report equity on a consolidated, or net, basis already. This figure was calculated by using this net data and data on equity issues found in Federal Reserve Bulletin Table 1.46. It also includes foreign direct investment in the US.
b. The data on trade credit in the UK suffers from incomplete coverage when compared to the data for the other countries. In the UK, this figure only covers part of advance payment for exports and some import credit. Other trade credits received by non-financial companies from other sectors of the domestic economy are not included. This underestimates total sources of funds for the UK in comparison with the other countries.
c. Provisions for pensions are what comprise this category for Germany. See discussion on pension provisions in the section on Germany below.

Sources: Own calculations from *Federal Reserve Board Flow of Funds Accounts Table F.102.* for the US, OECD Financial Statistics for Germany and France, Economic Planning Agency National Accounts for Japan, and Office of National Statistics Financial Statistics for the UK.

Uses of Funds

As mentioned above, significant differences exist in the patterns of uses of funds across financial systems. Exit-dominated financial systems were shown to invest a smaller share of total sources of funds than voice-dominated financial systems. In order to give greater detail to these patterns of uses, long-term averages for categories of uses of funds were calculated for the five countries for the entire period from 1970 to 1994.

These averages were calculated using the same weighting methodology as was described above for the calculation of the averages for sources of funds. These figures are reported in Table 2.4.

Table 2.4: Uses of funds: 1970–1994

Use	US	UK	Germany	France	Japan
Investment	57.4%	58.6%	77.1%	63.0%	70.4%
Bank Deposits	2.3%	8.9%	8.6%	7.4%	11.7%
Bonds	0.9%	1.3%[a]	2.4%	0.9%	1.0%
Equity	10.3%[b]	13.7%	2.8%	10.1%	0.8%
Trade Credit	10.1%	2.6%	12.3%	13.6%	13.9%
Other	19.0%	14.7%	6.8%	4.6%	3.2%

Notes:
a. This is a net figure for equity in the US. The Flow of Funds Accounts report equity on a consolidated, or net, basis already and no gross issues and purchases figures are available.
b. The UK figures do not include a separate category for the purchase of corporate bonds as a financial asset. This category includes British Government Securities and Northern Ireland Central Government Debt.

Sources: Own calculations from *Federal Reserve Board Flow of Funds Accounts Table F.102.* for the US, *OECD Financial Statistics* for Germany and France, *Economic Planning Agency National Accounts* for Japan, and *Office of National Statistics Financial Statistics* for the UK

These more detailed figures on uses of funds across financial systems support the claim made earlier based on the simple ratios of investment to total sources of funds. That is, voice-dominated financial systems use more of their funds for real investment than the exit-dominated financial systems. The exit-dominated systems purchase a larger amount of bonds and equities than Germany, Japan, and France. The figure for the purchase of equities in France stands out as being significantly larger than the other voice systems and closer to the levels found in the US and UK. This is also true for the investment figure in France. These figures are heavily influenced by the recent surge in the purchase of equities in France since the mid-1980s. This will addressed later in the section on France.

In sum, I argue that exit-dominated and voice-dominated financial systems can in fact be differentiated on the basis of uses of funds. Specifically, the US and the UK use a lower proportion of their funds for real investment than do the voice-dominated systems of Germany, France, and Japan. Although variations within the two groups do exist, with the US appearing to rely much more on bond finance than the UK[2] within the exit group and Japan relying much more on bank finance than Germany or

France within the voice group. There are, however, clear distinctions based on the extent to which the two groups rely on internal cash flow as a source of funds to finance physical investment and the extent to which they use funds for investment.   Others, like Jacobs (1994), confirmed the bank/market distinction between the two groups with data from the early 1970s and before. Clear distinctions can also be drawn when the data on the uses of funds is compared across the different financial system types. A necessary condition for convergence of these two types of systems would be for the voice-dominated systems to, over time, become increasingly dependent on cash flow and approach the level of internal finance seen in the exit systems of the US and the UK and reduce the proportion of funds used for investment. This book investigates how well these distinctions hold up over time when searching for evidence of convergence in international patterns of financing.

US

Sources of Funds

The Flow of Funds Accounts of the Federal Reserve were used to create the time series on sources of finance in the US. The sector examined was the non-farm, non-financial corporate business sector. This differs from the sectoral definition used in the OECD Financial Accounts. In OECD data, the farm sector and unincorporated businesses are included in the non-financial enterprise sector.

Time series of internal funds and bank finance as a share of net sources of finance are plotted in Figure 2.3. The internal finance as a share of net sources series shows a positive trend. Bank finance has also recently fallen as a share of net sources. As explained above, the US data on gross sources is not comparable to the other countries examined here and should be viewed with caution. However, the gross sources series on internal finance shown in the Appendix shows only a recent increase during the years 1991 to 1993 and a fall in bank finance over the same period. These three years account for the recent change in the gross sources of finance. The net shares series clearly suggest that the US is becoming even more dependent upon internal funds and is utilizing less bank finance over time. The gross series do not show such a clear trend but show a recent spike in the share of internal funds in gross sources and a fall in bank finance from 1991 to 1993.

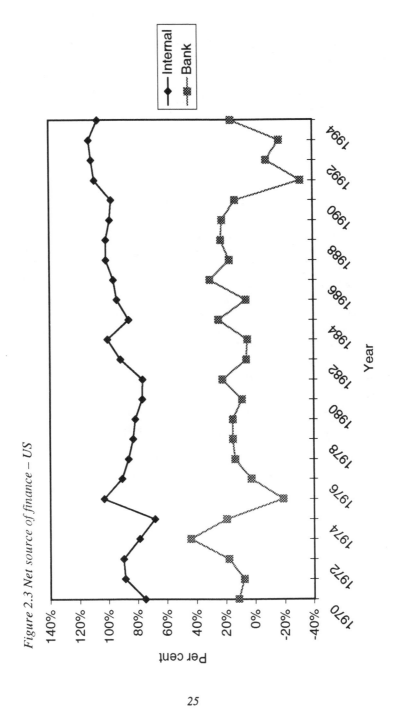

Figure 2.3 Net source of finance – US

In examining the net sources of finance for the US found in Table 2.5, a clear trend toward greater reliance on internal sources of funds emerges. Internal finance has increased as a share of net sources in every period except for a small decline from 87.8 per cent of net sources in the second half of the 1970s to 85.6 per cent in the first half of the 1980s. The statistical discrepancies in the second and fourth periods are quite high and suggest that the figures from these periods be viewed with some caution. The large negative values for the discrepancies in these two periods mean that there was a considerable amount of unidentified uses of funds in these periods. The net sources figures would change depending upon the distribution of these unidentified uses across the types of financial assets. The corporate mergers, buyouts, and stock re-purchases of the 1980s show up clearly in the net sources data. Firms borrowed both from banks and on the bond market to finance the repurchase of equity. Equity has been a net drain as a source of finance since 1980 as shown by its negative share of net sources in all three periods since then. Firms increased their reliance on bank financing in each period from 1975 to 1989 with bank finance providing 7.4 per cent of net sources from 1975 to 1979, 14.2 per cent in the first half of the 1980s, and 19.4 per cent of net finance from 1985-1989. Firms then increased their holdings of bank deposits to a greater extent than they increased their bank borrowing in the last period of 1990-1994, resulting in a –4.7 per cent net share for bank finance in that period. The US remains unique in its reliance on the bond market as a source of funds.

Table 2.5: Net sources of finance: US

Source	1970-74	1975-79	1980-84	1985-89	1990-94
Internal	79.6%	87.8%	85.6%	98.1%	107.2%
Bank Finance	21.1%	7.4%	14.2%	19.4%	-4.7%
Bonds	16.0%	14.9%	11.6%	23.7%	10.6%
Equity	7.4%	1.5%	-4.7%	-26.0%	-4.5%
Trade Credit	-2.8%	-8.2%	-7.3%	-5.5%	-0.5%
Other	-15.8%	7.1%	3.0%	9.4%	-6.7%
Discrepancy	-5.4%	-10.5%	-2.4%	-19.2%	-1.5%

Source: Own calculations from Federal Reserve Board Flow of Funds Accounts Table F.102.

Overall, the net sources data reflect an increasing reliance on internal funds. This makes the US a moving target with respect to the potential convergence of the voice-dominated countries. The heavily internally financed US financial system is becoming more reliant on retained earnings. Thus Germany, Japan, and France have that much further to go to converge to the level of reliance on internal finance found in the US.

Uses of Funds

The disaggregated uses of funds in five-year averages are presented in Table 2.6.

Table 2.6: Uses of funds: US

Use	1970-74	1975-79	1980-84	1985-89	1990-94
Investment	63.2%	59.6%	58.2%	48.2%	60.9%
Bank Deposits	3.0%	4.4%	1.9%	1.9%	1.1%
Bonds	0.1%	0.6%	1.7%	0.7%	2.0%
Equity	4.3%	4.4%	7.7%	18.7%	11.5%
Trade Credit	15.8%	15.9%	11.4%	7.9%	6.2%
Other	13.7%	15.1%	21.0%	23.7%	18.3%

Source: Own calculations from Federal Reserve Board Flow of Funds Accounts Table F.102.

There was a steady increase in the use of funds to purchase equities from the first period's level of 4.3 per cent to a level of 18.7 per cent in the period from 1985 to 1989. Over this same twenty-year period, investment and trade credit fell as a share of uses of funds. The US financial system re-purchased equities and invested less. This, as will be shown throughout the book, is a characteristic of the exit-dominated model.

UK

Sources of Funds

Time series of internal funds and bank finance as a share of net sources of funds for the UK are shown in Figure 2.4. The net series exhibit a good deal of stability from 1970 to the middle of the 1980s. Beginning in the middle of the 1980s and continuing until the end of the decade, internal finance fell as a net source of finance while bank finance increased as a net source. Then, in general, over the 1990s bank finance fell and internal funds increased as a share of net sources. The case of the UK differs from that of the US in that the UK data show no clear trend for internal funds as a

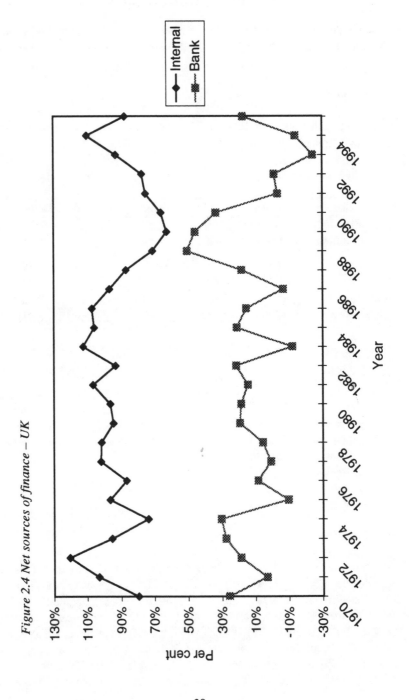

Figure 2.4 Net sources of finance – UK

share of financing whereas in the US there is a clear pattern of increasing reliance on internal funds when examined on a net basis.

The UK pattern of financing diverged from that of the US in the second half of the 1980s. As seen in Table 2.5, the US continued to increase the share of financing provided by retained earnings in the 1980s while the UK, as shown in Table 2.7, decreased the share of net sources of finance provided by internal sources. Recently, the UK has seen a fall in the internal finance share from 102.9 per cent in 1980 to 1984 to 81.2 per cent in 1985 to 1989 and a rise in the share of net sources provided by bank finance over the same two periods from 13.2 per cent to 29.1 per cent. The flows in the second half of the 1980s are illustrative of take-over activity in the UK whereby equity was purchased by the enterprise sector financed by bank borrowing. Bank finance increased in the period 1985 to 1989 while equity became an even greater net drain on financing. On a net basis, the enterprise sector in the UK increased their use of bank financing to purchase the sector's own equity shares to a greater extent than in any prior period. This pattern of financing flows reversed itself in the first half of the 1990s. The enterprise sector in the UK issued equity well in excess of its repurchase of equity shares so that equity became a positive net source of finance over the sub-period for the first time in the sample. Over the same sub-period, bank finance fell dramatically as a net source of finance, becoming negative for the first time.

Table 2.7: Net sources of finance: UK

Source	1970-74	1975-79	1980-84	1985-89	1990-94
Internal	91.0%	96.0%	102.9%	81.2%	83.4%
Bank Finance	23.4%	6.0%	13.2%	29.1%	-0.5%
Bonds	2.9%	0.0%	0.7%	6.6%	8.1%
Equity	–7.2%	–2.3%	–5.2%	–12.2%	9.6%
Trade Credit	–0.4%	–2.3%	–2.7%	0.1%	0.8%
Capital Transfers	6.8%	2.6%	2.8%	1.3%	0.8%
Other	6.6%	1.6%	–4.2%	4.9%	7.5%
Discrepancy	–23.1%	–1.5%	–7.4%	–11.0%	–9.7%

Source: All figures are based on author's calculations based on the Office of National Statistics Financial Statistics release obtained from the Data Archive at the University of Essex.

A notable pattern emerging from the figures on gross sources of finance in the UK shown in the Appendix is the steady increase in market (bonds and equity) sources of funds. This is particularly true with regard to equity but is also true for bonds with the exception of the slight decrease from the first half of the 1970s to the second half of the decade.

Uses of Funds

As discussed above in both the section on the long-term patterns of financing and the measures of investment as a share of gross sources of funds, the UK invests a lower proportion of its funds than do the voice-dominated systems. To examine how the pattern of uses of funds has changed over time in the UK, five-year averages of uses of funds were calculated. These figures are displayed in Table 2.8.

Table 2.8: Uses of funds: UK

Use	1970-74	1975-79	1980-84	1985-89	1990-94
Investment	53.8%	66.7%	61.5%	56.7%	55.9%
Bank Deposits	12.6%	7.4%	9.8%	8.2%	8.4%
Bonds[a]	0.1%	3.2%	1.7%	0.4%	1.3%
Equity	8.7%	8.0%	10.0%	18.2%	18.5%
Trade Credit	4.3%	5.9%	3.0%	0.8%	0.8%
Other[b]	13.7%	15.1%	21.0%	23.7%	18.3%

Notes:
a. Does not include corporate bonds but only British Government Securities.
b. Includes Other Investment Overseas, Other Overseas Financial Assets, and Unidentified Uses of Funds

Source: All figures are based on author's calculations based on the Office of National Statistics Financial Statistics release obtained from the Data Archive at the University of Essex.

Notably, since the second period in the 1970s, the share of funds going to the purchase of equities has increased in every period, from 8.0 per cent in 1975-1979 to 18.5 per cent in the period from 1990 to 1994. Investment has, over the same periods, fallen in every period, from 66.7 per cent in the period from 1975 to 1979 to 55.9 per cent in 1990-1994.

The UK remains a financial system in which finance is predominantly internal, although it has recently diverged somewhat from the US in its reliance on retained earnings. While the US has continued to increase its reliance on internal funds as a net source of financing, the UK has, in the last decade, reduced the share of internal funds as a net source of funds. However, this reduction still leaves the UK's use of internal sources of finance well above levels in the voice-dominated financial systems of Japan, Germany, and France. Thus, on the uses side, the UK has increased its purchases of financial assets and decreased the proportion of funds going to investment.

JAPAN

Sources of Funds

Figure 2.5 displays the time series of internal funds and bank finance as shares of net sources of funds. The net time series suggests a recent trend toward increased reliance upon internal funds and a decreased use of bank finance. As shown in the data on gross sources in the Appendix, bank finance represented a greater gross source of funds than did internal sources throughout most of the 1970s. Internal funds became a greater source of gross financing in 1977 and have remained a larger share of gross sources ever since. The shares of gross sources represented by internal funds and bank finance remained fairly stable until 1990. In 1990, internal funds began a rapid increase as a share of gross sources while bank finance declined quite considerably. This suggests a recent shift toward decreased reliance on bank finance and an increased reliance upon self-financing. The net sources of financing plots in Figure 2.5 reveal the same shift occurring in 1990, although the net shares of bank financing and internal funds were not as stable as the gross shares prior to 1990.

The figures on net sources of finance in Japan shown in Table 2.9 demonstrate that Japan has not converged in its pattern of financing to the US and UK model of heavy reliance on internal finance. It has, however, shown recent movement toward the exit-dominated system pattern. Internal finance increased as a share of net sources over each five-year period from the first half of the 1970s to the end of the 1980s. Internal funds as a share of finance increased from 55.5 per cent in the first period of the 1970s to 61.3 per cent in the second half of the 1970s, 67.1 per cent in the period 1980 to 1984, and 68.8 per cent in the last half of the 1980s. It has, however, fallen in the first half of the 1990s to 65.2 per cent of total net sources.[3] There is no convergence toward the extreme reliance on internal funds found in the US and UK. The highest net share of internal funds occurs in the period from 1985 to 1989 at 68.8 per cent.

Bank finance as a net source of funds in Japan has, in general, declined. It was at its highest level in the first period from 1970 to 1974 at 38.3 per cent of total net sources. Bank finance then fell as a net source in each period reaching a low of 17.2 per cent in 1985 to 1989 before increasing again to a level of 29.9 per cent in the last period. Judging from changes in the pattern of financing displayed in Table 2.9, Japan remains a

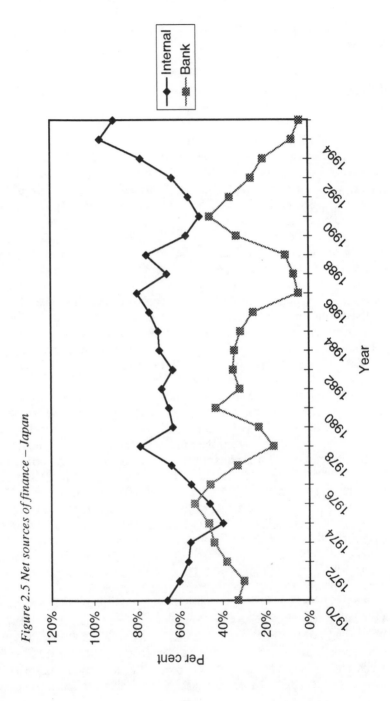

Figure 2.5 Net sources of finance – Japan

voice-dominated system. While internal finance has increased and bank finance has fallen as shares of net sources, they have not shown the changes that would be necessary to make the claim that Japan has completely converged toward the US – UK model of heavy reliance on cash flow. However, Japan has shown recent signs of movement toward the exit model pattern of financing and this movement is what we mean by convergence.

Table 2.9: Net sources of finance: Japan

Source	1970-74	1975-79	1980-84	1985-89	1990-94
Internal	55.5%	61.3%	67.1%	68.8%	65.2%
Bank Finance	38.3%	33.4%	34.9%	17.2%	29.9%
Bonds	6.3%	11.7%	5.2%	11.8%	7.9%
Equity	3.4%	3.9%	4.2%	3.7%	2.9%
Trade Credit	–6.5%	–8.3%	–6.5%	–4.3%	–1.8%
Other	2.9%	–1.4%	–5.0%	2.9%	–4.1%

Source: Own calculations from Economic Planning Agency of Japan, National Accounts, Table III.1: Capital Finance Accounts by Institutional Sector: Non-Financial Incorporated Enterprises.

The data on gross sources of finance in Japan found in the Appendix show clearer signs of convergence toward the pattern of financing found in the exit-dominated financial systems. Internal finance increased as a gross source of funds from a low of 32.4 per cent in 1970-1974 to 62.4 per cent in 1990-1994. This increase places Japan's share of internal funds as a gross source higher than that of the UK and approaching that of the US in the last period. Bank finance fell in every period except for the slight increase from 34.7 per cent to 36.0 per cent that occurred between the last period of the 1970s and the period from 1980 to 1984.

Another notable change in Japan's gross sources of finance is the decreased reliance upon trade credit. Trade credit declined as a gross source of finance in every period and has decreased sharply from the 1970 to 1974 level of 20.3 per cent to the 1990 to 1994 level of 0.7 per cent.[4] This decline did not show up in the net sources figures because, as will be seen in the next section on uses, trade credit also fell as a use of funds. The extensive historical use of trade credit in Japan has been a characteristic of the financial system that expanded the use of voice. Japanese firms with customers with close business relationships within or outside the corporate grouping would extend and be extended trade credit. The decline in trade credit on both the sources and the uses side signals a decline in the credit aspects of these relationships. Japan has converged toward the exit model of the US and UK with respect to the use of trade credit.

Uses of Funds

Two patterns emerge from examining the changing pattern of uses of funds in Japan found in Table 2.10.

Table 2.10: Uses of funds: Japan

Use	1970-74	1975-79	1980-84	1985-89	1990-94
Investment	55.2%	61.3%	70.0%	60.1%	95.6%
Bank Deposits	15.8%	14.1%	11.7%	21.8%	–4.5%
Bonds	0.3%	0.9%	0.7%	1.9%	0.6%
Equity	0.9%	0.8%	0.7%	1.9%	–0.9%
Trade Credit	26.0%	20.3%	14.8%	11.6%	2.6%
Other	1.6%	1.1%	–2.4%	6.3%	2.2%

Source: Own calculations from Economic Planning Agency of Japan, National Accounts, Table III.1: Capital Finance Accounts by Institutional Sector: Non-Financial Incorporated Enterprises.

Investment has, in general, increased as a proportion of uses while trade credit has declined as a share of uses of funds in every period. In the three periods from 1970 to 1984, Japan increased its investment while decreasing its liquid bank deposits and use of trade credit. In the period from 1985 to 1989, investment fell as a proportion of uses of funds from 70.0 per cent in the prior period to 60.1 per cent while Japan increased its liquid holdings from 11.7 per cent in the prior period to 21.8 per cent. In the 1990s, Japan dramatically increased its investment and drew upon liquid bank deposits and further reduced the use of trade credit.

Japan's pattern of financing, whether examined at the gross or net level, is still distinct from that found in the exit-dominated systems of the US and UK. It has, however, shown considerable change and movement toward greater reliance upon internal sources of funds and decreased reliance upon bank finance. This is particularly true when the pattern of financing is examined on a gross basis. The main characteristic of the Japanese pattern of financing that continues to distinguish it from that of the US and the UK is the fact that the Japanese enterprise sector does not purchase financial assets to the extent that the US and UK enterprise sectors purchase financial assets. In fact, Japan has, in general, increased the proportion of funds used for real investment. This is largely due to the decrease in the use of funds for trade credit. In the last period, bank deposits were drawn down and investment increased substantially. The purchase of large amounts of financial assets in the US and UK is what makes their net patterns of financing diverge from their gross patterns more than Japan's net pattern of financing diverges from its gross pattern. If the trends found in Japan's gross sources of financing continue and the Japanese enterprise sector begins to purchase financial assets at a higher level, then we will see a convergence of the Japanese pattern of financing toward the exit-dominated model when examined at the level of net sources of financing.

GERMANY

Sources of Funds

The non-financial enterprise sector of the German economy includes private and all public enterprises regardless of their legal form.[5] This is the widest sectoral definition of any of the five countries examined here. It includes public companies like the Federal Post Office and the Petroleum Storage Association and also includes partnerships if their transactions relate to production and capital formation. The inclusion of both public and unincorporated business in this sector makes this German sector uniquely broad and precludes exact sectoral comparability with other countries.

Another difficult issue in making international comparisons with the German financial system is the treatment of company pensions. German firms keep contributions to employee pensions on their balance sheets and are allowed to use the funds as they see fit. They can either plow the funds back into the enterprise or use them for investment or they can purchase financial assets. The problem lies in whether to treat these funds as debt, because they are a fixed liability which is senior in bankruptcy proceedings, or as part of internal funds, because the funds are generated within the firm and the firm is allowed to retain the funds and has discretion over them. In order to make this aspect of the German financial system clear, the funds that constitute pension provisions have been separated out in the sources of financing.

In examining the time series of internal sources of funds and bank finance as a share of net sources for Germany in Figure 2.6, there is no clear trend in either series. The same is true when examining the shares of gross sources of finance from internal sources and from banks that are shown in the Appendix. Both the gross and the net series exhibit variability. However, there is no trend toward increasing reliance on internal funds that

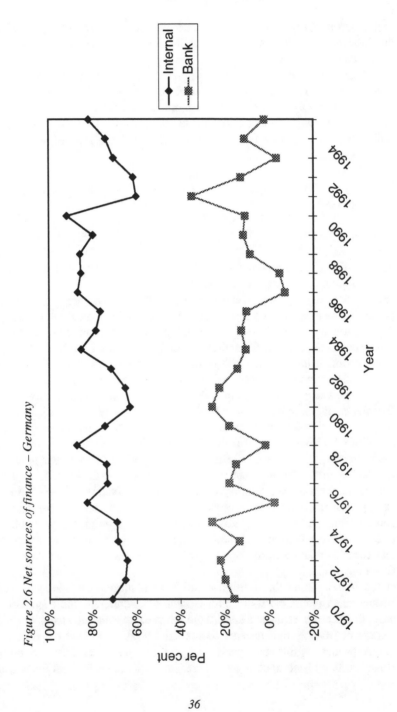

Figure 2.6 Net sources of finance – Germany

one would expect to find if the German system was converging toward the heavily internally financed exit model. Table 2.11 displays five-year averages of net sources of finance in Germany from 1970 to 1994.

Table 2.11: Net sources of finance: Germany

Source	1970-74	1975-79	1980-84	1985-89	1990-94
Internal	67.7%	77.9%	72.7%	82.8%	70.3%
Bank Finance	19.4%	11.3%	17.4%	4.1%	13.8%
Bonds	1.8%	–2.7%	–2.1%	0.6%	5.4%
Equity	0.7%	0.5%	–0.4%	2.4%	–3.4%
Trade Credit	–0.4%	–1.6%	–2.8%	–2.1%	1.3%
Capital Transfers	6.9%	9.4%	9.3%	7.9%	9.4%
Pension	3.9%	5.1%	6.0%	4.4%	3.3%

Source: Own calculations from *OECD Financial Statistics*

There is no trend toward greater reliance on retained earnings. In fact, internal finance has become less important in the last period. Internal sources of finance are more important in the latter period of the 1970s than the first half of the decade but then fall in importance from the second half of the 1970s to the first half of the 1980s. Retained earnings then increase again as a net source of funds, from 72.7 per cent of net sources in the early 1980s to 82.8 per cent in the period from 1985 to 1989. Notably, however, internal sources then fall to 70.3 per cent of net sources in the first half of the 1990s. There is no convergence toward the level of internal finance found in the US and UK. Movements in the share of bank finance in net sources of funds are opposite those of internal finance. There is no trend toward a decreased reliance on bank finance. Equity finance emerges as a significant net use of funds in the last period, with equity constituting –3.4 per cent of total net sources. This negative contribution of equity finance is a characteristic of the exit-dominated systems of the US and UK. The only real trend to emerge from Germany's changing pattern of finance is that bonds have steadily increased as a net source of funds from the second half of the 1970s. Bonds grew from being a net drain on financing, providing –2.7 per cent of the net sources over the 1975-1979 period to a net source providing 5.4 per cent of the net sources in the first half of the 1990s. In this respect the German system could be said to be becoming more similar to the US system, but bonds as a source of net funds will have to increase much more dramatically to match the 15.4 per cent average share that bonds provided in the US over the 1970–1994 period.

Gross sources of financing in Germany exhibit similar patterns over time as do net sources. There is no trend toward a decrease in the share of funds from bank finance or an increase in the share of funds provided by internal finance.[6] As in the net sources data, bond finance increases as a gross source from the second half of the 1970s to the most recent period.

Uses

The decomposition of uses of funds in Germany is presented in Table 2.12.

Table 2.12: Uses of funds: Germany

Use	1970-74	1975-79	1980-84	1985-89	1990-94
Investment	82.8%	78.8%	77.3%	77.2%	72.4%
Bank Deposits	11.7%	8.7%	5.9%	11.7%	6.4%
Bonds	0.3%	1.8%	2.1%	1.3%	4.8%
Equity	1.5%	1.7%	2.4%	1.2%	5.5%
Trade Credit	2.9%	3.9%	3.9%	2.2%	–0.1%
Other	0.8%	5.1%	8.2%	6.4%	10.9%

Source: Own calculations from *OECD Financial Statistics*

Germany's pattern of uses of funds reveals a declining share of funds being used for investment. Investment as a share of uses of funds has fallen in each period from a high of 82.8 per cent in 1970-1974 to a low of 72.4 per cent in 1990-1994. Germany has also shown a general trend of purchasing greater amounts of bonds and equities and of holding fewer funds as bank deposits. Germany deviated from this trend in the period from 1984 to 1989 when bank deposits increased and bonds and equities fell as a share of uses of funds. Another notable pattern on the uses side is the increase in the share of funds used for the 'other' category. This category is comprised of purchases of short-term and long-term loans. It is not clear from the OECD information, but this category is probably comprised of *Schuldscheinedarlehen* or 'certificates of indebtedness'. These are loans, not securities, but can be traded by transfer or assignment of title to the whole loan or part of the loan. These certificates of indebtedness are negotiable private placement promissory notes (Pozdena and Alexander 1987).

By the quantitative measures of net and gross sources of financing, there is no evidence of a convergence of the German financial system toward the pattern of financing exhibited by the US and UK. There is no tendency for internal funds to become increasingly important over time as either a gross or a net source. Also, there is no trend toward a decreased role for bank finance as a source of gross or net funds. Germany has not experienced the recent increased use of internal funds and decreased reliance on bank financing found in Japan. Therefore, by these measures of sources, there is no evidence in the German data of a convergence over time toward the exit model exemplified by the US and UK. On the uses side, Germany has shown a slow decrease in the share of funds going toward investment and a slow increase in the share used to purchase bonds and equities and other financial assets. While this is evidence of movement toward the pattern of fund use exhibited by the exit-dominated systems, Germany still invests a significantly larger share of total funds and purchases a significantly smaller proportion of financial assets than the exit-dominated systems of the US and UK.

FRANCE

Sources of Funds

The data for sources of financing for the non-financial enterprise sector in France comes from *OECD Financial Statistics Part 2, Financial Accounts of OECD Countries.* The sector includes public companies and private companies, as well as private non-profit institutions serving business enterprises.[7]

The time series of net sources of finance in France plotted in Figure 2.7 displays a trend toward increased reliance on internal finance and a decrease in the share of net finance provided by banks. There is a break in the relationship between bank finance and internal finance in 1984. This break also shows up in the time series plot of gross sources of finance shown in the Appendix. It is after 1984 that internal finance increases as both a net and a gross source and bank finance falls. The increasing share of finance provided by internal funds and the decreasing share provided by bank finance move the pattern of financing in the French system closer to the pattern of the exit-dominated systems of the US and the UK. The significance of 1984 as the inflection point at which internal finance rose and bank finance fell is discussed below.

The fact that the patterns of financing in the French financial system have showed a great deal of convergence toward the patterns of financing found in the exit-dominated systems of the US and UK can be seen in the five-year averages of net sources data in Table 2.13. Prior to 1984, internal

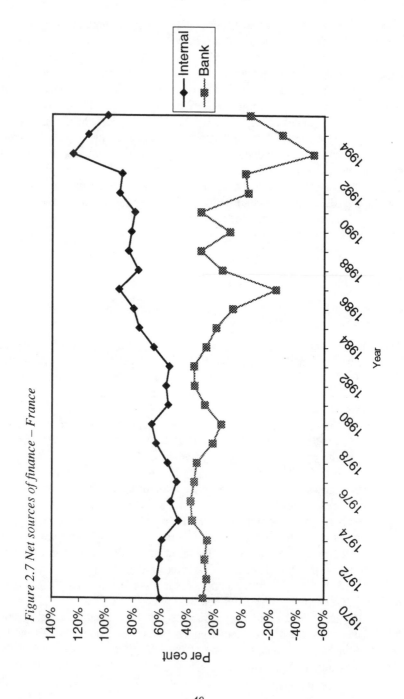

Figure 2.7 Net sources of finance – France

finance remained fairly low and stable, increasing from 57.3 per cent of net sources in the first period to 56.8 per cent in the last half of the 1970s and 60.0 per cent in the period from 1980 to 1984. In the last two periods internal finance has increased substantially.

Table 2.13: Net sources of finance: France

Source	1970-74	1975-79	1980-84	1985-89	1990-94
Internal	57.3%	56.8%	60.0%	82.2%	96.7%
Bank Finance	28.7%	26.5%	28.7%	9.2%	−7.9%
Bonds	4.2%	4.2%	5.4%	3.7%	5.5%
Equity	6.9%	8.9%	5.4%	5.8%	−2.2%
Trade Credit	1.6%	1.1%	−1.5%	−3.2%	0.9%
Capital Transfers	1.3%	2.5%	2.0%	2.3%	7.0%

Source: Own calculations from *OECD Financial Statistics*

Internal finance rose to 82.2 per cent of net sources in the last half of the 1980s to 96.7 per cent in the period from 1990 to 1994. This increase in internal financing has been accompanied by a pattern of decreased reliance on bank finance. When internal finance was stable, bank finance was also steady as a share of net financing. After 1984, however, bank finance fell from 28.7 per cent of net sources to 9.2 per cent in the period from 1985 to 1989 and fell again to −7.9 per cent from 1990 to 1994. The fall in bank finance has been almost entirely replaced by a rise in internal finance. Market sources of finance, bonds, and equity are actually less important as net sources of funds in the last period of 1990 to 1994 than in the period from 1980 to 1984. These combined market sources fell from 10.8 per cent to 2.3 per cent over these two periods. The French pattern of financing in the latest period is quite close to that of the US in the same period. Both exhibit a high reliance on internal finance, a negative value for bank finance and equity and a significant share of net sources of finance provided by bonds. This is evidence of a recent convergence of the French financial system.

It is noteworthy that the convergence has occurred after 1984. The 1984 Banking Act allowed for the creation of a money market for debt instruments of maturities of up to seven years. This was previously prohibited. After passage of the Act, banks were allowed to issue certificates of deposit, firms were permitted to float commercial paper, and commissions and fees for financial services were subsequently deregulated (Melitz 1990). This Act allowed all French banks to expand their business in the financial and insurance markets and become universal banks after which most stockbroking firms have been bought by the new universal banks (Bertero 1994). In 1986 a futures market on bonds was established. Melitz argues that the 'fundamental result of the general liberalisation is that the financial profile of France is now much more similar to the Anglo-Saxon model than it used to be' (Melitz, 1990 p. 398). The analysis of the French flow of funds data here provides evidence for this assertion.

The gross sources data shown in the Appendix also show an increase in internal finance and a fall in bank finance after 1984. However, the gross sources show a large increase in equity as a share of gross finance. This large increase in equity as a gross source coupled with the decrease in equity as a net source show that firms have increased their issuance of equity but have increased their purchase of equity as a financial asset at an even greater rate. Bonds have not exhibited a trend toward providing a larger share of gross sources. France shows clear signs of convergence toward the exit model at the gross level with bank finance being replaced by internal funds and equity finance.

Uses of Funds

Table 2.14 shows the decomposition of the uses of funds in France over the entire period.

Table 2.14: Uses of funds: France

Use	1970-74	1975-79	1980-84	1985-89	1990-94
Investment	80.5%	70.2%	56.2%	59.5%	58.4%
Bank Deposits	11.8%	9.6%	7.4%	4.4%	6.2%
Bonds	0.3%	0.5%	0.9%	1.3%	1.1%
Equity	1.4%	1.9%	6.5%	13.7%	19.8%
Trade Credit	5.3%	15.3%	23.0%	14.0%	8.3%
Other	0.6%	2.7%	6.0%	7.1%	6.0%

Source: Own calculations from *OECD Financial Statistics*

Equity purchases in France have increased in every period from a low of 1.4 per cent in 1970-1974 to a high of 19.8 per cent in 1990-1994. Investment as a share of uses of funds has fallen from a high of 80.5 per cent in 1970-1974 to 58.4 per cent in 1990-1994. The holding of bank deposits and related liquid assets has fallen from 11.8 per cent of total uses in the first period to 6.2 per cent in 1990-1994. France has changed its pattern of uses of funds in such a way that by the last period its pattern of fund usage is nearly identical to that of the UK (see Table 2.10).

In terms of both sources and uses of funds, France has shown significant convergence toward the exit pattern of financing, particularly after the financial reforms of 1984. France has exhibited dramatic reductions in its reliance upon bank finance and an increased reliance upon internal finance. In addition to these changes, the non-financial enterprise sector of the French economy has begun to purchase financial assets and invest less out of total funds. This change is further evidence of convergence of the French financial system toward the exit model of the US and UK.

CONCLUSION

An important finding of this chapter is that financial systems differ both in their composition of financing sources and in the composition of their uses of funds. This argument has not previously been put forth in the literature on financial systems. This chapter showed that the exit-dominated financial systems of the US and UK use a smaller portion of their sources of funds for investment than do France, Germany, and Japan. It also showed that these exit-dominated systems purchase a larger amount of financial assets as a share of total sources of funds than do the voice-dominated financial systems.

NOTES

1 The US data on equity is already a net figure. Gross issues and gross purchases of equities are not given in the Flow of Funds Accounts. An estimate of the gross figures can be made by using the net figure from the *Flow of Funds Accounts* and the figures on equity issuance found in Table 1.46 of the *Federal Reserve Bulletin*. This figure can then be compared with the net equity figures from the *Flow of Funds Accounts* to calculate the gross purchases of equity (gross issues − gross purchases = net equity).

2 The fact that the bond market in the UK is shown to be a smaller net source of funds than in the US can perhaps be partly explained by the fact that the flow of funds data for the US does not show acquisitions of corporate bonds as financial assets as a separate item. They are included in the residual 'Other' category on the asset side. This prevents a proper netting with respect to corporate bonds in the US and exaggerates the size of the US bond market as a net source of funds. However, judging from gross issues of corporate bonds, it is safe to say that the US bond market is a larger gross source of finance than in the UK (Corbett and Jenkinson 1994, p. 9). The question of the relative net contribution of the bond market cannot, however, be answered due to limitations in the data.

3 When the unweighted series plotted in Figure 2.7 is examined, an increase in internal finance and a decrease in bank finance can be seen in the last three years. Since these years are periods

of low total funds being raised, the weighted averages in Table 2.11 show a decline in internal funds.

4 See Appendix.

5 See OECD Financial Statistics Methodological Supplement, 1990.

6 See Appendix.

7 Bertero (1994) calculates net sources of finance for France up to 1992 exclusive of public and quasi-corporate public enterprises and arrives at shares of net sources that differs in some magnitudes but shows similar trends with respect to internal and bank finance.

APPENDIX

The difficulty in making comparisons based on gross sources data for the US have already been discussed. The increase in internal finance does not show up until the last period when considering the gross sources in Table 2.6. The share of internal finance in gross sources remains relatively steady, varying from a low of 51.8 per cent in the first period to a high of 54.1 per cent from 1980 to1984. The only significant increase comes in the last period when retained earnings increase from 53.7 per cent of gross sources in the last half of the 1980s to 72.7 per cent in the period from 1990 to 1994. No other clear trends emerge from the gross sources data, and the problems with these data make the net sources calculations a much more reliable gauge of the pattern of financing in the US.

Table A2.1: Gross sources of finance: US

Source	1970-74	1975-79	1980-84	1985-89	1990-94
Internal	51.5%	51.9%	50.5%	48.1%	66.1%
Bank Finance	16.5%	8.3%	10.2%	10.6%	−1.8%
Bonds	10.5%	9.1%	8.5%	11.5%	8.4%
Equity	5.7%	3.3%	4.6%	4.1%	7.9%
Trade Credit	13.2%	9.6%	4.2%	3.9%	6.1%
Other	2.6%	17.7%	22.0%	21.8%	13.3%

Notes: Equity figures are estimated by using gross equity issuance data from *Federal Reserve* Bulletin Table 1.46

Source: Author's calculations from *Federal Reserve Board Flow of Funds Accounts Table F.102* and *Federal Reserve Bulletin Table 1.46*

Table A2.2: Gross sources of finance: UK

Source	1970-74	1975-79	1980-84	1985-89	1990-94
Internal	58.8%	72.5%	69.4%	49.8%	58.1%
Bank Finance	25.9%	13.4%	20.0%	27.6%	5.8%
Bonds	1.9%	0.0%	0.5%	4.0%	5.6%
Equity	2.7%	5.1%	6.2%	9.8%	19.2%
Trade Credit	3.4%	3.3%	1.1%	0.9%	1.7%
Capital Transfers	4.4%	2.0%	1.9%	0.8%	0.6%
Other	3.0%	3.8%	0.9%	7.1%	9.1%

Source: Author's calculations from Office of National Statistics Financial Statistics release obtained from the Data Archive at the University of Essex.

Table A2.3: Gross sources of finance: Japan

Source	1970-74	1975-79	1980-84	1985-89	1990-94
Internal	32.4%	36.6%	46.5%	41.6%	62.4%
Bank Finance	37.1%	34.7%	36.0%	29.8%	24.3%
Bonds	3.9%	8.0%	5.8%	7.2%	8.3%
Equity	2.9%	3.2%	3.6%	4.5%	1.8%
Trade Credit	20.3%	16.2%	10.3%	10.2%	0.7%
Other	3.2%	1.1%	−2.4%	6.3%	2.2%

Source: Author's calculations from Economic Planning Agency of Japan, National Accounts, Table III.1: Capital Finance Accounts by Institutional Sector: Non-Financial Incorporated Enterprises.

Table A2.4: Gross sources of finance: Germany

Source	1970-94	1975-79	1980-84	1985-89	1990-94
Internal	55.5%	61.1%	56.3%	64.1%	50.9%
Bank Finance	28.2%	23.0%	27.6%	21.1%	27.4%
Bonds	1.8%	–0.3%	0.5%	1.7%	8.7%
Equity	2.2%	2.2%	2.0%	3.0%	3.1%
Trade Credit	3.6%	2.8%	1.7%	0.6%	0.8%
Capital Transfers	5.7%	7.4%	7.2%	6.1%	6.8%
Pension	3.2%	4.0%	4.7%	3.4%	2.4%

Source: Author's calculations from *OECD Financial Statistics*

Table A2.5: Gross sources of finance: France

Source	1970-94	1975-79	1980-84	1985-89	1990-94
Internal	46.3%	39.3%	33.8%	49.6%	55.0%
Bank Finance	35.4%	31.3%	29.5%	16.9%	8.3%
Bonds	3.7%	4.1%	4.0%	3.5%	4.2%
Equity	7.0%	7.2%	9.5%	16.9%	19.3%
Trade Credit	6.6%	16.3%	22.1%	11.8%	9.2%
Capital Transfers	1.1%	1.9%	1.1%	1.4%	4.0%

Source: Author's calculations from *OECD Financial Statistics*

3. Financial Systems and Investment

INTRODUCTION

Beginning with Keynes (1936), Kalecki (1937) and continuing with Minsky (1975) and others, models of investment behaviour have been developed where investment is determined by the demand and supply price of the investment good. In these models, the demand price (P_D) is the present value of profit flows or quasi rents a firm expects to earn from a marginal investment. The level of investment the firm will undertake is determined by where the demand price for the investment good is equal to the supply price a firm must pay for that marginal investment. One factor affecting P_D in this literature is capacity utilization as some measure of output demand. When excess capacity grows, the present value of future profits from the investment good decreases. This leads to a fall in P_D after some level of investment. Other reasons for P_D to be concave with respect to investment have been put forward. Keynes (1936, Ch. 16) and Davidson (1972, p. 72) discuss how, as investment rises beyond some point, the return on investment falls because the reduction in the scarcity of that capital good reduces the quasi-rent earned by the investment. Importantly for this book, this literature has also viewed financial conditions to help determine the demand price for capital. Keynes (1936, Chs. 11,12), Kalecki (1937, pp. 105-23), and Minsky (1975, Ch. 5; 1986, Ch. 8) discuss how a firm's investments can be financed by its own internal funds or externally by taking on debt. Any investment undertaken in an amount greater than the firm's internal funds creates future interest obligations for the firm. The cost of this external financing rises with the level of investment.

This phenomenon was called the 'principle of increasing risk' by Kalecki (1937) and 'lender's risk' by Keynes (1936). Both claimed that lenders would demand higher interest rates as investment by the firm increases. Kalecki argued this premium would be charged because the danger of illiquidity rises with the scale of the investment project. For Keynes, the premium was due to the possibility of default due to moral hazard by the borrower or the disappointment of their expectations.[1] Minsky (1975) decomposed Keynes' concept of lender's risk into borrower's risk and lender's risk. Borrower's risk is the risk of failure to meet debt commitments that causes the buyer of a capital asset to lower the demand price for that asset to compensate for the increased default risk due to borrowing. Lender's risk depends on the 'margin of security' for the loan, which is viewed as the lender's expectation of the amount the firm's future income will exceed payments required to service the loan. Both borrower's and lender's risk increase with the level of external financing in Minsky's model. This causes P_D to fall when investment exceeds the amount that could be financed internally. The speed with which P_D falls depends on the leverage ratio of the firm with the demand price falling more rapidly the more leveraged the firm is. This approach focuses solely on the leverage ratio as determining borrower's and lender's risk. I extend this model of investment behaviour to take into account the effect various institutional arrangements for obtaining external finance have on the degree of borrower's and lender's risk. Specifically, I examine how the institutional relationships like those found in voice-dominated financial systems serve to diminish borrower's and lender's risks.

THE STANDARD TWO-PRICE MODEL

The two-price model below is from Blecker (1997) and is an adaptation of Minsky (1975). In this model of investment, P_I and P_K are the supply price and demand price of investment goods. The supply price depends on the production costs and the costs of short-term finance for working capital and is constant up to the point where capacity is exceeded in the investment goods sector and supply constraints increase this supply price. The demand price of investment goods is determined by the present discounted value of expected future profits from investment. This model differs from Minsky's in that he assumed P_K to be constant. Here, I follow Mott (1982) who posits that the demand price can fall after the point where additional investment would surpass the amount anticipated to be required to keep pace with the future growth of the market. Here, the level of investment is determined by the intersection of P_S and P_D that deviates from P_I and P_K due to lender's and borrower's risk respectively. The curve FF represents the firm's expected amount of internal financing. It is a rectangular hyperbola in P, I space because the amount of investment that the firm can finance internally is given by F, the amount of expected internal funds, divided by the price of the investment good. This relationship is expressed as I=F/P and thus F=IP(I) is a rectangular hyperbola in P-I space. The amount of investment

I_1 will be financed internally while the amount I^*-I_1 will be financed externally. With no financial constraints, that is with no borrower's or lender's risk, the amount of investment would be determined by the point where P_I and P_K intersect (I_0). The presence of borrower's and lender's risk causes investment to be lower than it would be in their absence. It is in this sense that post-Keynesians view investment to be financially constrained.[2]

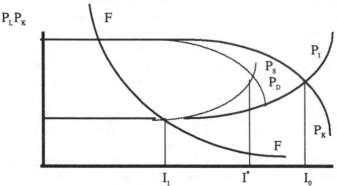

Figure 3.1 The standard two-price model

Blecker (1997) demonstrates how in this theory of investment, changes in corporate savings or cash flow, represented by the FF curve, are likely to be correlated with investment. A shift out in the FF curve causes both borrower's and lender's risk to decline because it permits the firm to finance any given amount of investment with less borrowing. The firm is then in a better position to cover its cash commitments on the borrowing if the returns to its investment disappoint its expectations. The P_s and P_D curves shift out as a result of this increased internal finance reducing borrower's and lender's risk with the result being a higher level of investment.

BORROWER'S AND LENDER'S RISK AND FINANCIAL STRUCTURE

This approach to investment behaviour has been successful in explaining the independent effect of internal finance on investment. However, it has not taken into account the possibility that different institutional arrangements for securing external finance might affect this relationship. That is, this approach has not examined the ways in which borrower's and lender's risk may be influenced by financial structure. Working from this tradition, a theory of investment that considers the effects of different institutional arrangements for financing must argue that different institutional arrangements for financing investments are likely to affect borrower's and lender's risks and hence investment activity. In this framework, both borrower's risk and lender's risk are understood to be uniformly increasing with respect to the leverage ratio of a firm. The higher the borrowing in relation to internal finance used to finance investment, the higher the level of borrower's and lender's risk. I argue that this is not a relationship that holds uniformly across firms or across financial systems. Firms with closer ties to banks or countries with voice-dominated financial systems are able to tolerate a higher degree of leverage, are able to borrow to a greater degree, because of the particular institutional arrangements they have for financing investment.[3] This model of investment behaviour is adapted so that it takes into consideration how the institutional arrangements for carrying out external financing can impact on investment. It does this by assuming that borrower's and lender's risk can vary across firms that are embedded in distinct financial systems. Specifically, the institutional relationships between firms and their lenders, as well as other specific financing arrangements in voice-dominated financial systems, lower borrower's and lender's risks. The institutional arrangements for carrying out firm financing in these systems relax the financing constraints on firms.

Borrower's Risk

How might borrower's risk be influenced by the different institutional arrangements for external financing found in different financial systems? Again, borrower's risk is the risk the borrower foresees of failing to meet debt commitments. The cash commitments the firm makes arising from borrowing are certain while the cash flows from the capital assets it finances with this debt are uncertain. There is some risk that the cash flow of the firm will fall short of being able to meet the debt commitments arising from borrowing. A firm in this situation is said to be in financial distress. This risk of borrowing causes firms to lower their demand price for capital assets in order to compensate for this default risk. What the firm cares about is that, if this happens, the failure to meet debt commitments may result in bankruptcy. So one can decompose borrower's risk, the risk the firm faces by borrowing, into the risk of failing to meet its debt commitments, default risk or the risk of financial distress and the conditional probability of financial distress resulting in bankruptcy, or bankruptcy risk. There seems to be no reason for firms with different relationships with banks or embedded in different financial systems to face differing default risks. Firms face a fundamental risk that the cash flows they expect from their investments will not be forthcoming to the degree they had hoped. This is a fundamental risk of operating that can't be insured against. Some ventures fail. I argue, however, that firms with close ties to banks or, at the macro level, the average firm in voice-dominated financial systems, will have a lower risk of the failure to meet debt commitments resulting in bankruptcy. That is, they will have a lower risk of default resulting in bankruptcy and thus a lower level of borrower's risk.

Why is the risk of bankruptcy lower, resulting in a lower level of borrower's risk, in voice-dominated financial systems where firms have close ties to banks? In general, it is the ability of firms with close ties to banks to renegotiate the financial claims on the firm with those banks in times of financial distress. Financial distress is the default scenario discussed above. It occurs when firms are unable to meet their debt commitments. Firms with close ties to banks are more likely to be able to renegotiate these financial commitments with lenders and remain going concerns. Banks with close ties to firms may be more willing to renegotiate financial claims with firms because these close ties mitigate some of the information and incentive problems of financial distress.

If these close ties produce better information, then firms will have an easier time convincing a closely tied lender that they really are viable in the long run if existing financial claims can be renegotiated.[4] If creditors are numerous and dispersed, then a collective action problem among the creditors may result in times of a debtor's financial distress. Bulow and Shoven (1978) and Gertner and Scharfstein (1990) point out that free-rider problems reduce the incentive for creditors to grant financial relief or extend credit since an individual creditor bears the full costs of such relief but shares the benefits. No creditor will have an incentive to renegotiate for fear other creditors will free ride.

Bankruptcy law in the US and the UK inhibits banks from forming close ties to their customers. This is in addition to the prohibition against owning equity stakes in commercial firms. In the UK, a financial firm is liable as a 'shadow director' for any advice that contradicts the objective of minimizing the potential loss of all the company's creditors. In the US, if a bank is found to exercise effective control over a debtor firm, the bankruptcy court's penalty may be a significant reduction in the priority status of the bank's claims as a creditor.[5] These laws thus punish banks that form close relationships with their borrowing customers and have the impact of reducing the willingness of banks to participate in informal corporate rescues (Frankel and Montgomery 1991). US law further impedes informal workouts by prohibiting binding votes by bondholders to change the principal amount, interest rate, or maturity date of a bond.[6]

Suzuki and Wright (1985) provide evidence for this relationship between close bank ties and default risk when they show that in times of financial distress companies in Japan that have strong ties to banks are more likely to avoid bankruptcy proceedings than companies that lack main bank ties. The 'main bank' system of Japan, in which a main bank is delegated the role of monitoring the firm and takes the lead in renegotiating the financial claims of a firm in financial distress, diminishes collective action and information problems and thus makes renegotiation more likely.[7] The fact that the main bank is delegated the role of taking the lead in the renegotiation reduces the co-ordination problem that would exist if a renegotiation were attempted with many creditors simultaneously. These renegotiations may include a refinancing or a rolling over of existing debt, forgiving principal payments, interest rate reductions or the provision of bridge financing.   Sheard (1992) describes these sorts of 'workout' arrangements between Japanese firms and their main banks, who take the lead in these processes. White (1996) discusses how debt renegotiations are also relatively easy for large firms in Germany. This is because major bank lenders tend to be represented on firms' boards of directors and there is less reliance on publicly traded debt, thus making the number of parties that must agree on a voluntary restructuring relatively small.[8]   These relationships may thus reduce the cost of financial distress.[9]

These sorts of arrangements reduce the probability that a bad outcome, the shortfall of cash flows to meet debt commitments, will result in a bankruptcy and the failure of the firm. These arrangements result in lower levels of borrower's risk. Firms with close ties to their banks still face the fundamental risk of their cash flows being insufficient to service their debt. However, these firms have mitigated the risk of this default resulting in bankruptcy by forging close ties with their lender.

This makes a firm that has this sort of relationship with its lender more willing to take on debt than a firm that does not. This can be shown by adapting the Minsky framework so that these relationships which lower the conditional risk of bankruptcy are factored into borrower's risk. We can do this by assuming that if P_D, the demand price of capital assets, decreases as borrower's risk rises.   This risk can be further understood as being decomposed into the fundamental risk of default and the conditional probability of this default resulting in bankruptcy.   The close ties with lenders found in voice-dominated systems like Japan, Germany, and France operate on the conditional probability of bankruptcy.   A lower risk of default resulting in bankruptcy lowers borrower's risk. This means that P_D falls away from P_K more slowly for a firm that, everything else equal, has ties to its lender which mitigate the risk of borrowing resulting in failure.

In Figure 3.2, P_D' reflects the lower level of borrower's risk that a firm would face if it had close links to its lender that mitigated the conditional risk of bankruptcy. P_D reflects the higher level of borrower's risk faced by a firm without close ties to its lender. Bankruptcy risk need not increase with leverage at the same rate for firms with different relationships with their lenders.

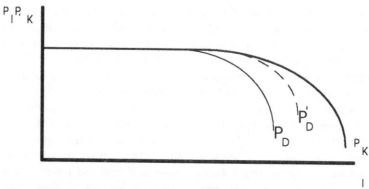

Figure 3.2 Borrower's risk and ties to lender

Thus, two firms with the same anticipations of future cash flows resulting from an investment and facing the same cash commitments resulting from borrowing can have different levels of borrower's risk. Their different levels of borrower's risk arise from their different institutional arrangements for financing the investment.

Lender's Risk

Keynes discussed how in an economy with borrowing and lending certain risks arise, one of which is lender's risk.

> But where a system of borrowing and lending exists, by which I mean the granting of loans with a margin of real or personal security, a second type of risk is relevant which we may call the lender's risk. This may be due to either a moral hazard i.e. voluntary default or other means of escape, possibly lawful, from the fulfilment of the obligation, or the possible insufficiency of the margin of security i.e. involuntary default due to the disappointment of expectation. (Keynes, 1936 p. 144)

Lenders run the risk of their loans not being repaid. They lend on the expectation that the debt a borrowing firm takes on can be serviced from the future cash flows the borrowing firm generates. Lenders want protection from this risk and the demand for this protection shows up in the financing conditions that lenders set. Minsky (1975) lists higher interest rates, shorter terms to maturity, and restrictions on dividend payouts and further borrowings as forms in which lender's risk shows up on financial contracts.

Much of the lender's risk comes from potential agency costs of debt. Jensen and Meckling (1976) describe this agency problem of debt. Agency costs of debt arise when there is an incentive for managers of the borrowing firm to act in their own interest or that of equity holders and against the interest of creditors. Myers (1977) describes the particular problem of 'debt overhang'. This problem has to do with the fact that firms in financial distress may under-invest because they may be unable to finance potentially profitable investments since much of the benefits of the new investment accrue to existing debt-holders. That is, potential suppliers of new funds are reluctant because much of the benefit of the new investment may flow to existing holders of more senior claims on the firm. Again, in Myers' framework lender's risk is understood to rise as the leverage ratio of a firm increases and there is no mention of different institutional arrangements for lending and borrowing affecting lender's risk. The close ties between firms and banks in voice-dominated financial systems, with banks holding equity in the firms to which they lend, may mitigate the agency problem of debt. It may mitigate this agency problem in such a way that would lower lender's risk and thereby provide a greater quantity of available lending and allow firms in financial distress to have greater access to new financing.

Prowse (1990) shows evidence of the idea that the agency problem of debt is mitigated to a greater degree in Japan than in the US. He does this by demonstrating that debt ratios of US firms are negatively related to the firm's potential to engage in risky investments whereas Japanese debt ratios show no such relationship.

External Finance and Internal Finance

If borrower's and lender's risks are lower, then P_s and P_D will fall away from P_I and P_K more slowly.[10] This is shown in Figure 3.3 with $P_s{}'$ and $P_D{}'$ representing the lower levels of lender's and borrower's risk that we assume are characteristic of voice-dominated financial systems where firms and banks have closer ties. The result is a higher level of investment (I^{**}) and a greater portion of investment being financed externally ($I^{**} - I_1 > I^* - I_1$). As discussed above, increases in cash flow cause the FF curve to shift out to the right and decrease borrower's and lender's risk. This decrease in risk results in a movement of the P_s and P_D curves closer to the P_I and P_K curves, causing investment to increase.

Similarly, decreases in cash flow would result in higher levels of borrower's and lender's risk and a reduction in investment. Thus cash flow and investment are positively correlated. Voice-dominated systems and exit-dominated systems will exhibit different responses to equivalent changes in cash flow. Voice-dominated systems display lower levels of borrower's and lender's risk and levels of investment that are closer to the unconstrained level represented by the intersection of the P_I and P_K curves. Therefore, equivalent changes in cash flow have a smaller impact on borrower's and lender's risk in voice-dominated systems than in exit-dominated systems.

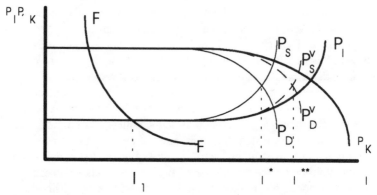

Figure 3.3 Borrower's and lender's risk in the two systems

This means external finance will behave differently across financial systems. This is because of the different levels of borrower's risk and lender's risk and the different resulting cash flow elasticities of risk, or the different degrees of responsiveness of borrower's and lender's risk to changes in cash flow. External finance will be positively correlated with internal finance in exit-dominated systems and will be less positively correlated and potentially negatively correlated with internal finance in voice-dominated systems. To illustrate this, imagine equivalent reductions in cash flow in each type of system. A reduction in cash flow in an exit-dominated system results in a significant increase in borrower's risk and lender's risk. This is shown graphically in Figure 3.4. The FF curve shifts left to FF' and the increased risk causes P_S and P_D to shift inward as well to P'_S and P'_D. The fall in cash flow has resulted in a fall in investment from I^* to I^{**} and a fall in external finance. External finance falls because (I^*-I_1) is greater than $(I^{**}-I_2)$. In the model of an exit-dominated financial system, a fall in cash flow is associated with a reduction in investment and a reduction in external finance. Cash flow is positively correlated with investment and external finance. The reduction in cash flow will result in a smaller increase in borrower's risk and lender's risk in voice-dominated financial systems. Graphically, this means that for an equivalent shift to the left of FF to FF' the demand and supply curves for investment shift in to the left by a smaller amount than was the case in the exit model above.

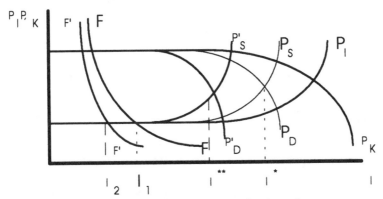

Figure 3.4 A reduction in cash flow in an exit-dominated system

In Figure 3.5, investment has also fallen but by less than in the model of the exit-dominated financial system. Investment has fallen from I^* to I^{**} and the amount of external finance has increased. External finance has increased because $(I^*-I_1) < (I^{**}-I_2)$. In this case, external finance and cash flow are negatively correlated.

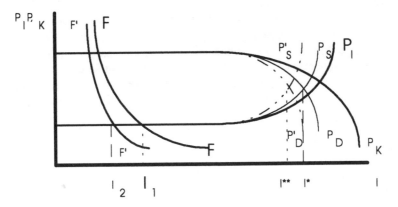

Figure 3.5 A reduction in cash-flow in a voice-dominated system

The intuition behind these two models is that in voice-dominated financial systems closer ties between firms and lenders lead to lower levels of borrower's and lender's risk. Banks help firms smooth their sources of investment financing by providing external finance when it is most needed in times of lowered internal finance. In exit-dominated systems, external finance is positively related to cash flow, but if banks help to smooth investment in voice-dominated systems, then external finance will be less positively correlated, uncorrelated, or negatively correlated with cash flow. Banks with closer ties to firms in voice-dominated systems may be more willing to provide financing to firms that are facing cash flow reductions. Firms in exit-dominated systems facing reductions in cash flow are likely to see reductions in their ability to obtain external financing until their cash flow increases.

Liquidity

I have suggested that the institutional arrangements in financial systems impact on the level of borrower's and lender's risk and that these differences produce different relationships between internal finance, external finance, and investment. Differences in financial systems, I argue, also produce differences in the liquidity of firms. This has to do with the way in which the firm (or the non-financial business sector) uses its funds. I argue that exit-dominated financial systems or firms without close ties to lenders will use more of their funds for the purchase of liquid assets. They will be more liquid and less willing to undertake fixed investment than firms with close ties to lenders or voice-dominated financial systems which invest more in fixed assets.

Liquid financial assets provide a low-cost source of investment financing in exit-dominated financial systems where firms face higher levels of risk in borrowing and more volatile loan flows. It has already been suggested that in exit-dominated systems external finance will be more positively correlated to internal finance and more volatile than in voice-dominated systems. In exit-dominated financial systems, accumulated liquid financial assets can be used as a cushion that may reduce the sensitivity of investment to cash flow variability. Firms with an uncertain availability of flows of external finance may accumulate financial assets as a form of precautionary saving to help smooth investment over periods of reduced cash flow.[11]

This argument can also be illustrated by using the adapted Minsky framework developed above. The Minsky framework does not allow for the possibility that firms will simultaneously borrow and purchase financial assets. Firms either borrow in excess of cash flow or invest the sum of cash flow and lending, or they invest less than their cash flow and use the excess cash flow to purchase financial assets or retire debts. With these limitations in mind, the model can still be adapted to demonstrate why firms in exit-dominated financial systems are more likely to invest less and purchase more financial assets than firms in voice-dominated systems.

As in Figure 3.3, assume that the higher level of borrower's risk in an exit-dominated financial system causes the demand price for investment goods conditional on the level of borrower's risk to fall more steeply from the unconditional demand price than is the case in voice-dominated systems. For simplicity we will abstract from the difference across financial systems in lender's risk and thus the conditional supply price of investment goods and assume the same supply price of investment in each type of system.

Figure 3.6 displays the scenario for financing investment for both financial system types assuming the same levels of cash flow and supply functions for investment goods. The only difference between the two systems is the level of borrower's risk. The level of borrower's risk is higher in the exit-dominated system causing, as discussed above, the demand price for investment goods conditional on borrower's risk P_D^e to fall away from the unconditional demand price P_D more quickly than is the case in the voice system's conditional demand illustrated by P_D^v.

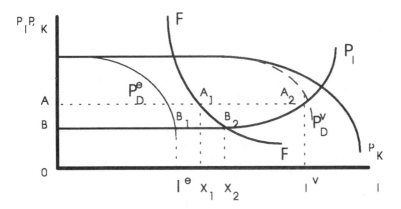

Figure 3.6 The impact of different levels of borrower's risk

The two levels of investment in the two systems, I^e for the exit-dominated system and I^v for the voice-dominated system, illustrate two possible extremes with respect to the impact of different levels of borrower's risk. In the exit-dominated system the level of borrower's risk is high enough to push investment demand below the level that could be financed internally. Therefore the residual cash flow is used to purchase financial assets and no borrowing takes place. The amount spent on investment is OBB_1I^e and the value of financial assets purchased in the exit-dominated system is $I^eB_1B_2X_2$. Investment is higher in the voice-dominated system with the quantity of investment demanded represented by I^v. The amount spent on investment in the voice system is $0AA_2I^v$. In order to finance this level of investment, borrowing is required. Internal funds in the amount of $0AA_1X_1$ is used and $X_1A_1A_2I^v$ is borrowed. No financial assets are purchased in the voice system. In this model, the exit-dominated system invests less, borrows less (nothing), and purchases more financial assets than the voice-dominated system. We would not expect such extreme cases to be the norm empirically. There is likely to be both borrowing and financial asset purchases in both systems. However, as discussed above, this model does not allow for the possibility of both borrowing and purchasing financial assets. It does allow us to illustrate two extreme cases that serve to bracket the possible financing patterns. The model shows exit systems investing less, borrowing nothing and purchasing financial assets and the voice system investing more, borrowing, and purchasing no financial assets. Empirically we would expect the non-financial enterprise sector in exit systems to invest less, borrow less, and purchase more financial assets than the same sector in voice systems. Unlike in the model, however, we would expect the non-financial enterprise sector in voice-dominated systems to purchase some financial assets and the sector in exit-dominated systems to engage in some borrowing.

This propensity for exit-dominated systems to purchase financial assets as well as problems of aggregation suggest that, unlike at the firm level, at the macro-level, voice-dominated financial systems are likely to have a tighter relationship between sources of funds and investment. This includes a tighter relationship between cash flow and investment because these voice-dominated systems invest more of their sources of funds. At the firm level, a tighter relationship between cash flow and investment would be expected for financially constrained firms. One might then expect exit-dominated financial systems to show a tighter relationship between cash flow and investment. However, at the sectoral level, when all firms are aggregated, it is not the sector as a whole bumping up against a financial constraint that we are looking for in the relationship between cash flow and investment. Some firms are likely to be financially constrained and others are not and when we aggregate across firms this effect will be washed out.[12] Instead of detecting a financial constraint, what we will be detecting at the sectoral level in the relationship between flows of financing (including cash flow) and investment is how much of that incremental flow of financing is going to investment. If exit-dominated systems are more liquid and use this stock of liquid financial assets to help smooth the fluctuations in cash flow and volatile flows of external finance, then they are likely to have a weaker relationship between investment and flows of finance like cash flow.

Several propositions regarding the different relationships between the behaviour of investment, cash flow, and external finance flow from the model developed here. They are:

1. External finance will be more positively correlated with cash flow in exit-dominated financial systems and perhaps even negatively correlated with cash flow in voice-dominated financial systems thus making external finance more volatile in exit-dominated systems.[13]
2. Internal finance will be a greater source of investment financing in exit-dominated systems.
3. Investment will be higher in voice-dominated financial systems.
4. Investment will be less volatile in voice-dominated financial systems.
5. Investment is more closely related to flows of financing in voice-dominated systems because of the greater propensity of firms in exit-dominated systems to purchase financial assets. This is related to the nature of external financing referred to in the first proposition.

Evidence regarding these propositions as they relate to the financial systems of the US, UK, France, Germany, and Japan is presented in the following two chapters.

NOTES

1 Lender's risk, Keynes argued, 'may be due to moral hazard, i.e. voluntary default or other means of escape, possibly lawful, from the fulfillment of obligation, or to the possible insufficiency of the margin of security'(Keynes 1936, p. 144).

2 Blecker (1997) points out how this specific understanding of financial constraints - that the level of investment permitted by the conditions of finance is less than the level which would be consistent with the projected growth of demand and the supply conditions for investment goods - differs from asymmetric information credit-rationing models.

3 The differences between the level of the firm and the macro-level of a country's financial system are important. This book deals mostly with differences across countries at the macro-level. However, differences also exist across firms within financial systems. For example, Petersen and Rajan (1994) discuss the benefits to small firms of relationships with lenders within the exit-dominated financial system of the US. They find that ties between small firms and their lender increases the availability of financing and have a smaller effect on the price of credit. Hoshi, Kashyap, and Scharfstein (1990) investigate differences across firms within the voice-dominated financial system of Japan. They find that investment by firms with close ties to banks is less sensitive to liquidity than it is in the case of firms that lack close ties to banks.

4 Hoshi, Kashyap, and Scharfstein (1990) argue that when debt is held diffusely, bondholders are not likely to be well informed about the firm and may not know whether it is profitable to provide new capital or to give interest and principal concessions.

5 This is known as the concept of equitable subordination in US bankruptcy law.

6 US bondholders (dispersed creditors) are prohibited from renegotiating with the firm in a way that is binding by the Trust Indenture Act. See Roe (1996) for an examination of this prohibition. Individual bondholers, may, however voluntarily exchange their bonds for new issues with lower interest rates, principal amounts, or different maturities.

7 Hoshi (1994) discusses how the main bank system in Japan reduces this collective action problem.

8 White (1996) refers to a German language study on bankruptcy in Germany.

9 Hoshi, Kashyap, and Scharfstein (1990) find that financially distressed firms that are members of a corporate group in Japan or have close ties to a bank invest more than non-group firms and firms without close ties to banks in the years following the onset of financial distress.

10 Minsky (1975) allowed for the possibility that borrower's risk and lender's risk could differ across firms and account for different rates of investment. However, his story for these differences is one based on subjective differences not institutional differences. He writes: 'The fundamental fact about both borrower's and lender's risks is that they reflect subjective valuations. Two entrepreneurs facing identical objective circumstances but having different temperaments would view the borrower's risk quite differently...'(p.110). He also discussed how leverage ratios can change through time over the business cycle dependent on how subjective assessments of borrower's and lender's risks change (1975 p. 111; 1986 p. 190).

11 The possibility of this occuring at the firm level is discussed by Fazzari, Hubbard, and Petersen (1988). They find that a stock measure of liquidity has a greater impact on the investment of firms that are more likely to be financially constrained.

12 Mott (1982) discusses the difference between his cross sectional studies and his time series studies of the relationship between investment, cash flow, and debt. Due to the common problem of aggregation, some of the relationships that he finds in the cross sectional data are not found in the time series data.

13 Jacobs (1996, Essay III) thought the leverage ratio would have lower cyclical variability in BB countries but it did not. He was trying to test Minsky's financial instability hypothesis across countries. Jacobs is confusing the issue by using the leverage ratio that has investment in the denominator and financial liabilities in the numerator because investment has different variances across countries independent of changes in financial liabilities.

4. External and Internal Finance

In general, it has been found that external finance is procyclical in the US. Calomoris, Himmelberg and Wachtel (1995) found that commercial paper issuance is procyclical at the firm level and Perry and Schultze (1993) found that short-term credit flows were negative around the troughs of three of the last four recessions. Friedman and Kuttner (1993) also found that negative earnings shocks cause bank loan volume to fall. This evidence suggests a positive relationship between internal funds and external funds in the US. Carpenter, Fazzari, and Petersen (1994) argue these findings suggest that short-term debt does not offset reductions in internal finance during downturns. If, in a downturn, cash flow falls and external financing do not make up for this fall in internal sources of financing, then there will be less financing available for investment and investment will fall.

Is this a universal relationship holding across financial systems or across firms? Or, is it a distinctive feature of the exit model and firms without close ties to lenders? The argument presented in this chapter is that the institutional arrangements in voice-dominated systems create a different environment for the provision of external finance. In voice-dominated systems, firms can use external finance to smooth investment. That is, as opposed to the procyclical nature of external finance for the US described above, external finance is likely to be acyclical or countercyclical in voice-dominated systems. When cash flow falls, firms with close ties to banks or countries with voice-dominated financial systems are able to offset this fall in internal sources of financing with external financing and thus smooth the total sources of funds available for investment and investment itself.

To investigate whether the relationship between internal finance and external finance differs across financial systems, time series of cash flow and bank finance of non-financial enterprises were calculated from flow of funds data. The first point to make about differences in the behaviour of bank finance across countries is that the flow of bank finance is considerably more volatile in exit-dominated financial systems than in voice-dominated systems. This can be seen by examining the standard deviations of the growth rates of bank finance flows over the entire period. These are reported in Table 4.1.

Table 4.1: Volatility of bank finance: 1970–1994

Country	Volatility of Bank Finance
Japan	0.230
Germany	0.440
France	0.881
UK	0.970
US	1.309

Note: Volatilities measured as the standard deviation of the growth rate of flows of bank finance over the period.

Clearly, the exit-dominated financial systems have a higher volatility of bank finance. Bank finance is least volatile in Japan followed by Germany, France, the UK, and the US. The exit-dominated systems have bank finance volatilities that are nearly five times as high for the UK and over six times as high in the US as those in Japan. The growth rate series for France is particularly interesting in that it displays a significant break in 1984, the time of major financial deregulation in France.[1] The standard deviation of the growth rate in France prior to 1984 was 0.266 while it was 1.156 in the period following deregulation.

Perhaps bank finance is more volatile in exit-dominated systems because cash flow is more volatile in these systems. To help investigate this possibility, volatilities of internal funds were calculated for the five countries. They are reported in Table 4.2.

Table 4.2: Volatility of internal funds: 1970–1994

COUNTRY	Volatility of Internal Funds
Japan	0.142
Germany	0.124
France	0.100
US	0.090
UK	0.148

Note: Volatilities measured as the standard deviation of the growth rate of flows of real internal funds over the period.

The volatility of internal funds is roughly equivalent across the five countries. Thus, the higher variability of bank finance cannot be easily explained by a higher variability of internal funds. However, it is possible that bank finance has a different relationship to internal funds across financial system types.

In order to examine further this possibility, regressions involving bank finance, cash flow, and output were run. First, these series were tested for stationarity. These series were found to be non-stationary in levels but stationary in first differences.[2]

Time series of the first differences of gross bank finance and internal finance for the US are shown in Figure 4.1. From the plot it appears as if there is a positive relationship between these two series. The same positive relationship appears in the plot for the same two series for the UK in Figure 4.2. That is, as internal funds fall, bank finance also falls. These same first differences for Germany are shown in Figure 4.3. Here, these two series appear to show a negative relationship. As internal finance falls, bank finance tends to increase. The plot of the first differences of bank finance and internal finance for France shown in Figure 4.4 shows no significant relationship between the two series. From Figure 4.5, bank finance and internal finance also appear to have no significant relationship in Japan.

The relationships evident in the time series plots are confirmed by calculations of correlation coefficients between the first difference of internal finance and the first difference of bank finance. These correlation coefficients are shown in Table 4.3.

Table 4.3: Cash flow – bank finance correlations: 1970–1994

Country	Correlation Coefficient
Japan	0.07
Germany	– 0.22
France	0.02
UK	0.24
US	0.40

Note: Correlation between first difference of real flows of bank finance and internal finance of non-financial enterprise sector.

Source: Own calculations from *OECD Financial Statistics Part 2* and *Federal Reserve Board Flow of Funds Accounts* for the US.

Cash flow and bank finance are positively correlated in the US and the UK, negatively correlated in Germany and nearly uncorrelated in France and Japan. This is consistent with the model's predictions regarding the relationship between external finance and internal finance across financial

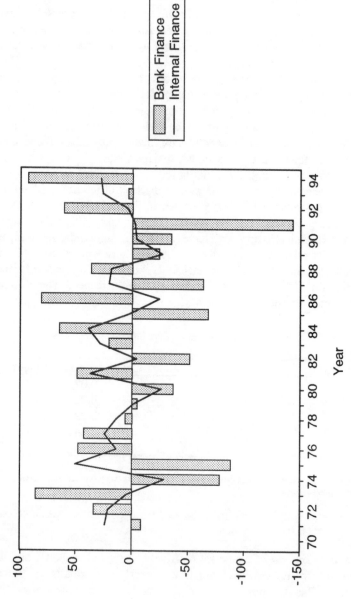

Figure 4.1 First differences of gross bank finance and internal finance - US

Figure 4.2 First differences of gross bank finance and internal finance - UK

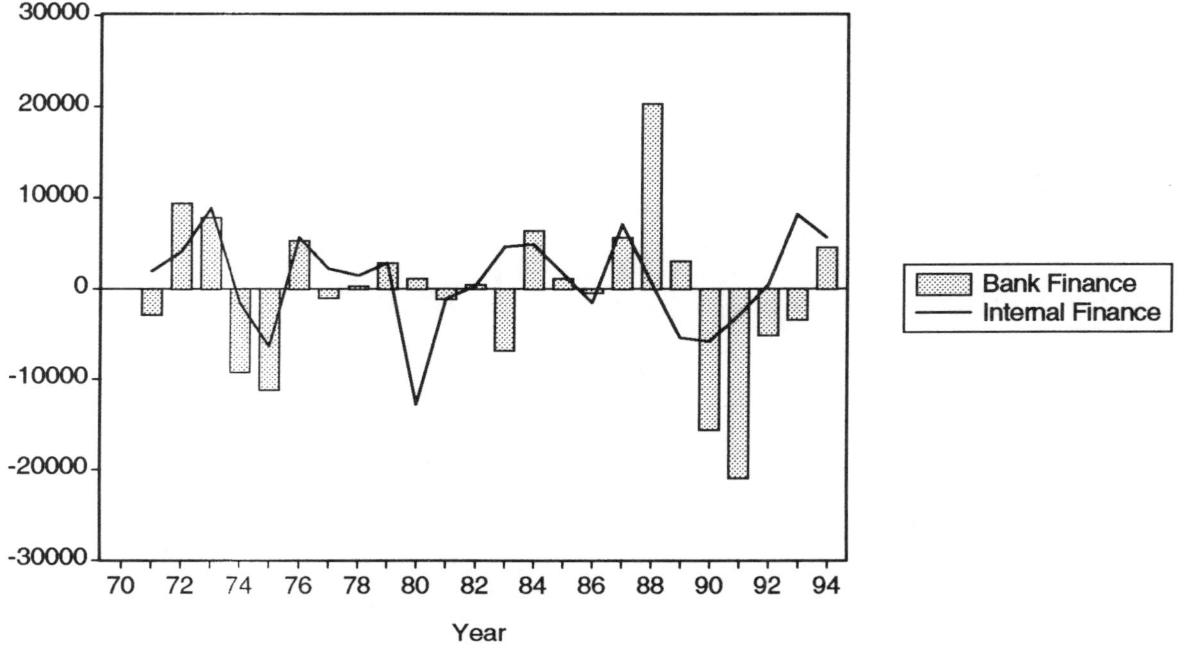

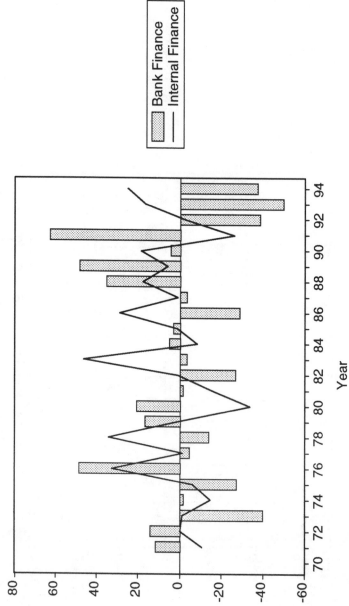

Figure 4.3 First differences of gross bank finance and internal finance - Germany

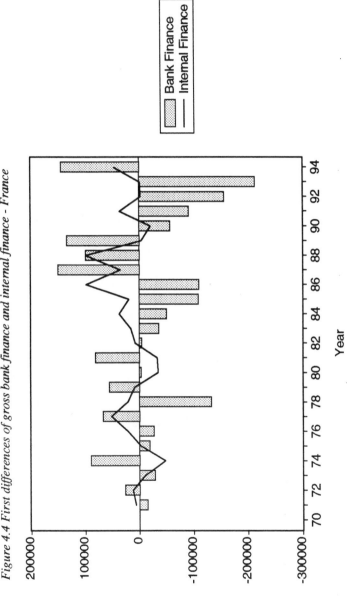

Figure 4.4 First differences of gross bank finance and internal finance - France

Bank Finance
Internal Finance

Year

69

Figure 4.5 First differences of gross bank finance and internal finance - Japan

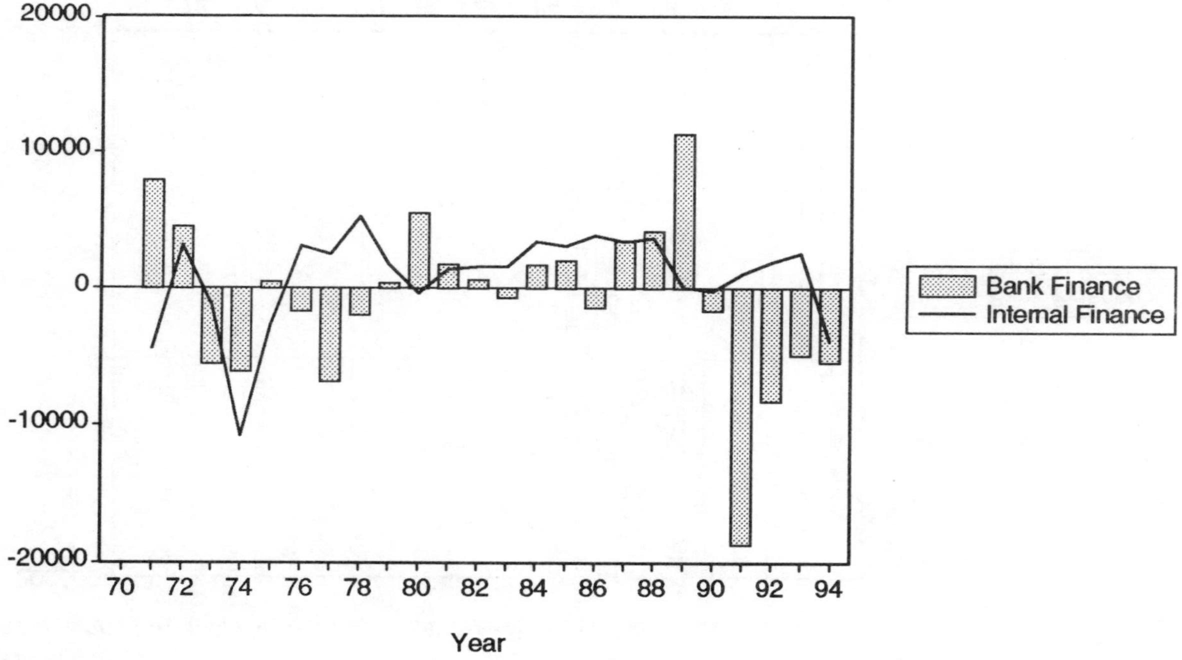

Year

Bank Finance
Internal Finance

systems. In exit-dominated financial systems like those in the US and UK with higher degrees of borrower's and lender's risk, we would expect to see falls in internal finance met with reductions in flows of external finance as the reduction in internal funds causes a significant increase in risk. Falls in internal finance in voice-dominated systems result in smaller increases in risk because the institutional arrangements in these systems serve to mitigate these risks. This results in smaller reductions in external finance and perhaps even increases in external finance as firms draw on their lenders to help smooth total sources of funds as internal sources fall. This is evident in the relationship between internal funds and bank finance in Germany. France and Japan exhibit almost no correlation between internal finance and bank finance. Still, all that is needed to sustain the argument that external finance is used to smooth investment in voice-dominated financial systems to a greater extent than in exit-dominated systems is that the relationship between internal finance and bank finance is less positive in these systems than in exit-dominated financial systems. This argument is consistent with the evidence on the correlations between bank finance and internal finance across countries. Countries with exit-dominated financial systems exhibit more positive correlations between bank finance and internal finance than countries with voice-dominated financial systems.

In order to investigate further the different relationships between external bank funds and internal funds across countries, regressions were run on the differenced series of gross bank finance and internal finance for each country. The regression results suggest a more positive relationship between gross bank finance and cash flow for the US and UK than for the other countries. This is consistent with the simple correlation coefficients reported above.

To further investigate the relationship between bank finance and cash flow across financial systems, a multivariate regression was run on the first differences of bank finance, cash flow, real gross national product, and investment for each of the five countries. The output variable is used as a control to see if cash flow and investment have any independent impact on the flow of bank finance, controlling for changes in output. If bank finance is more costly than internal funds and is the preferred means used to fund the gap between internal funds and desired investment, then demand for bank finance can increase as cash flow falls and/or investment increases. The cash flow coefficients for all of the voice-dominated systems are negative while they are positive for the exit-dominated systems. This suggests that as cash flow falls in the voice-dominated systems, bank finance increases to fill the gap while bank finance and cash flow move together in exit-dominated systems. These multivariate regression coefficient estimates vary across countries with respect to their precision.[3]

The evidence in this chapter shows that cash flow is of roughly equivalent volatility across financial systems while bank finance is more volatile in exit-dominated systems. This data also shows that there is a stronger positive relationship between cash flow and bank finance in exit-dominated financial systems. This is all evidence in support of the claim that bank finance serves more of a smoothing function in voice-dominated financial systems than in exit-dominated systems. To further examine this claim, volatilities of the sum of cash flow and flows of bank finance were calculated. The sum of these two flows is referred to as ready funds. The volatilities of ready funds are reported in Table 4.4:

Table 4.4: Volatility of ready funds: 1970–1994

Country	Volatility
Japan	0.098
Germany	0.122
France	0.185
UK	0.250
US	0.220

Notes: Volatilities measured as the standard deviation of the growth rate of the sum of flows of real bank finance and real internal funds over the period.

First, these volatility measures show that the voice-dominated systems have a lower volatility of ready funds. Second, when these volatilities are compared with the cash flow volatilities reported in Table 4.2, bank finance has made ready funds more volatile than cash flow for the exit-dominated systems of the US and UK while it has made ready funds less volatile than cash flow alone in Germany and Japan. That is, bank finance has helped smooth the sources of funds available for investment in Germany and Japan while it has made these sources more volatile in the exit systems of the US and UK. This is both the product of the higher volatility of bank finance in exit countries and the difference in the relationship between bank finance and cash flow across countries. This can be seen from the formula for the variance of the sum of two variables:

$$\mathrm{Var}(CF + BF) = \mathrm{Var}(CF) + \mathrm{Var}(BF) + 2\mathrm{Cov}(CF, BF) \qquad (4.1)$$

The variances of cash flow were similar across countries while bank finance was more volatile in exit systems. If these two variables were unrelated, then the higher cash flow volatility found in the exit-dominated systems would alone cause these systems to have a higher volatility of ready funds.

However, the positive relationship between these two flows in exit systems makes bank finance exacerbate the volatility of cash flow in these systems. Because of the negative relationship between cash flow and bank finance in voice-dominated financial systems, bank finance can actually smooth ready funds, the sum of cash flow and bank finance. This is what is observed in the data shown in Table 4.4.

France once again displays a significant break in 1984 due to the increase in the volatility of bank finance since the 1984 deregulation. Prior to 1984 bank finance made ready funds less volatile than cash flow while after 1984 it has made it more volatile. When considered over the entire period, the post-1984 period outweighs the impact of the pre-deregulation period and, overall, bank finance has made ready funds more volatile than cash flow in France.

The results of both the bivariate and multivariate regressions as well as the measures of the volatility of bank finance, cash flow, and ready funds indicate that bank finance behaves differently across financial systems. Exit-dominated financial systems have a higher level of bank finance volatility and a stronger positive relationship between cash flow and bank finance than do voice-dominated systems. In addition, bank finance and investment are more strongly related in voice-dominated systems. These findings support the view presented at the begining of this chapter that bank finance helps smooth the funds available for investment in voice-dominated financial systems by being less positively tied to cash flow or perhaps even making up for deficiencies in cash flow. Again, all that is needed to suggest that bank finance helps smooth investment in voice-dominated systems to a greater degree than in exit-dominated systems is that the bank finance – cash flow relationship be more strongly positive in exit-dominated systems than in voice-dominated systems. The evidence presented here is stronger than this. It suggests that in voice-dominated sytems, bank finance and cash flow are negatively related.

NOTES

1 See the section on France in Chapter 2 for more detail on the deregulation.

2 Schaberg (1997) contains the full econometric results.

3 Only the regression for Germany has a statistically significant coefficient on cash flow at the 5 per cent level. For Germany, the relationship between bank finance and internal finance is negative. While Germany is the only regression that has a statistically significant coefficient on cash flow at the 5 per cent level and the first regression for Japan performs poorly with no detectable relationship between bank finance and cash flow, one-sided tests of the cash flow coefficients for the other regressions yield useful results. A one-tailed test indicates that the cash flow coefficient for the second specification for Japan is negative at the 4.5 per cent level and the cash flow coefficient for France is negative at the 19.0 per cent level of significance. The same

coefficient for the UK is positive at the 22.6 per cent level of significance. Similarly, the cash flow coefficient estimate for the US is positive at the 26 per cent level of significance.

APPENDIX

Regressions investigating the relationship between cash flow and bank finance were run using the equation:

$$BF_t^k = C + b_1 CF_t^k \qquad\qquad (A4.1)$$

Where BF is the first difference of flows of gross bank finance to the non-financial business sector of country k at time t, C is a constant term, and CF is the first difference of cash flow for the same sector in country k at time t. The results of the regression are reported in Table A.1.

Table A4.1: Gross bank finance – cash flow regressions

Country	C	CF	R^2	D.W.
Germany	1.252	-0.313	0.001	1.763*
	(6.242)	(0.317)		
France	–9325	–0.067	–0.044	1.726*
	(22069)	(0.579)		
Japan	–918.1	0.145	–0.038	1.090
	(1305)	(0.372)		
Japan AR(1)*	–1816	0.153	0.123	1.702*
	(1964)	(0.370)		
UK	–1022	0.674	0.124	1.424*
	(1657)	(0.325)*		

Notes
a. A regression with an AR(1) term was run for Japan to correct for the presence of positive serial correlation. Dependent variable is real investment.
b. All variables are in first differences and standard errors are in parenthesis.
c. * indicates statistical significance at the 5 per cent level and

The Durbin–Watson test statistics show that there is no serial correlation problem except for Japan. Another regression was run for Japan with an AR(1) correction to remove the serial correlation. The regressions yield negative coefficients on the cash flow variables for Germany and France, a slightly positive coefficient for Japan, and larger positive coefficients for the US and UK. This is consistent with the simple correlation coefficients reported above. The coefficient estimates are not very precise as indicated by their standard errors, except for the UK that has a statistically significant positive coefficient at the 5 per cent level. However, these standard errors allow us to perform one-sided tests and infer that the coefficient on internal finance in the US is positive at the 13.7 per cent level of significance and that the coefficient on internal finance in Germany is negative at the 16.6 per cent level of significance while those of Japan and France are not statistically significantly different from zero.

The multivariate regressions examining the relationship between cash flow and bank finance were of the form:

$$BF_t^k = C + b_1 CF_t^k + b_2 Y_t^k + b_3 I_t^k \tag{A4.2}$$

The results of these regressions are reported in Table A.2.

Table A4.2: Regressions of gross bank finance on cash flow, output, and investment

Country	C	CF	Y	I	R^2	D.W. Stat.
Germany	−4.445	−0.521*	191.3	0.642*	0.416	2.103*
	(7.116)	(0.248)	(277.3)	(0.241)		
France	−11715	−0.500	154319	0.928*	0.177	2.154*
	(41938)	(0.553)	(161998)	(0.460)		
Japan	−4568.5	−0.161	106929	−0.075	–	1.226
	(2870.8)	(0.416)	(777356)	(0.335)	0.01	
Japan[1]	731.3	−0.551	−50767	1.156**	0.500	1.572*
	(2265.6)	(0.309)	(57347)	(0.255)		
US	−27.25	0.311	926.3	0.674	0.252	2.555*
	(15.93)	(0.531)	(596.3)	(0.828)		
UK	−2830	0.246	98792	0.801	0.422	1.754*
	(1785)	(0.353)	(89209)	(0.611)		

Notes
a. A regression with an AR(1) term was run for Japan to correct for the presence of positive serial correlation.Dependent variable is real investment.
b. All variables are in first differences and standard errors are in parenthesis.
c. A * indicates statistical significance at the 5 per cent level and
d. A ** indicates significance at the 1 per cent level.

None of the regressions display serial correlation problems except for the first regression for Japan. A second specification was used for Japan to try to correct for the serial correlation. This specification used investment with a lead of one period instead of contemporaneous investment. The superiority of this specification for Japan suggests that there is a more pronounced gap between the flow of investment financing and the undertaking of investment in Japan. All of the regressions for the voice-dominated systems, except for the first specification for Japan, have statistically significantly positive coefficients on the investment variable. This suggests that bank finance will increase to help fund increases in investment. The exit-dominated systems don't exhibit as strong a relationship in this regard.

5. Investment, Financial Asset Purchases and Sources of Funds

THE COMPOSITION OF INVESTMENT FINANCING

The model developed in Chapter 3 suggests that countries with voice-dominated financial systems, where firms have closer ties with banks, will rely on external finance to a greater extent than countries with exit-dominated financial systems, where internal finance will provide a greater source of investment financing. Evidence on the composition of investment financing in the five countries considered here is consistent with this result of the model.

The Level of Investment

The model's suggestions regarding the reduction in borrower's and lender's risk in terms of the level of investment are supported by evidence that levels of investment are higher in countries with voice-dominated financial systems. Considering investment levels from 1975 to 1994, Japan, Germany and France have had higher levels of investment than the US or UK. Figure 5.1 displays time series of gross domestic investment as a share of output for these countries. The average levels of investment as a percentage of output are given in Table 5.1.

By this measure, Japan has the highest level of investment followed by France, Germany, the US, and the UK. This ranking holds for longer periods as well.[1] All of the investment series were tested for stationarity. Only the series for Japan was found to be stationary as the presence of a unit root was rejected at the 1 per cent significance level.

How does the level of investment at the level of the economy as a whole relate to the financial systems and the patterns of financing in these countries? The first important point to make is that the US and UK use a considerably lower proportion of total gross sources of finance for real investment. In the exit-dominated financial systems, firms purchase more

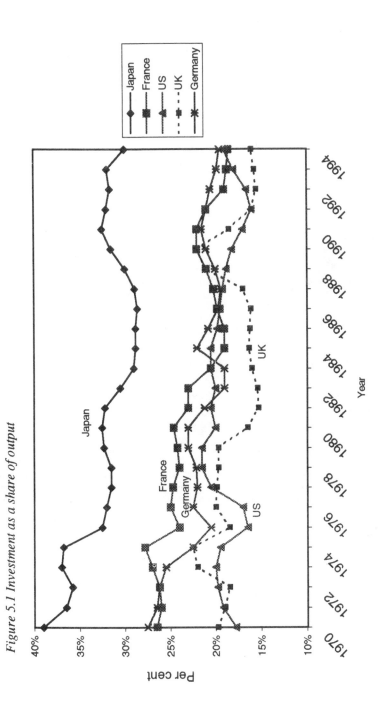

Figure 5.1 Investment as a share of output

financial assets and invest less with the funds that they raise than in the voice-dominated systems. The voice-dominated financial systems of Germany, France, and Japan invest a higher proportion of their funds and purchase fewer financial assets.

Table 5.1: Investment as a share of output: 1970–1994

Country	Average Share	Std. Deviation
Japan	30.1 %	0.017
Germany	21.0 %	0.011
France	21.5 %	0.020
UK	17.7 %	0.019
US	18.7 %	0.018

Table 5.2 gives the average of the ratio of real investment to total real gross sources of funds for the five countries over the period 1970 to 1994.

Table 5.2: Investment as a share of total gross sources: 1970–1994

Country	Average Share	Std. Deviation
Japan	69.0 %	0.210
Germany	78.9 %	0.073
France	65.9 %	0.110
UK	58.2 %	0.083
US	49.6 %	0.094

Source: Own calculations from *OECD Financial Statistics Part 2* for France and Germany, *Economic Planning Agency National Accounts* for Japan, *Office of National Statistics Financial Statistics* for the UK, and *Federal Reserve Board Flow of Funds Accounts* for the US.

As with investment as a share of output, the non-financial enterprise sectors in countries with voice-dominated systems also invest more out of their total gross sources of funds than is the case in the exit-dominated financial systems of the US and UK. In these exit-dominated systems, the business sector invests less and purchases more financial assets out of total sources of funds.

FINANCIAL ASSET PURCHASES: PRECAUTIONARY AND SPECULATIVE

Why have the non-financial enterprise sectors of the countries with exit-dominated financial systems invested less and purchased greater amounts of financial assets than their counterparts in countries with voice-dominated systems? There are two possible motives for the higher levels of financial asset purchases in countries with exit-dominated financial systems derived from Keynes' discussion of motives for saving (Keynes 1936): the precautionary motive and the speculative motive.

The basic argument for the precautionary motive for the purchase of financial assets is that agents accumulate assets to cope with unexpected drops in income. Keynes (1936) used this argument to explain one of the reasons individuals save. Following Keynes, a literature on precautionary saving has developed that focuses on personal saving and consumption behaviour. This literature began with Friedman (1957). The notion that individuals increase their saving in order to deal with the uninsurable risk of earnings uncertainty has been explored both empirically and theoretically (Leland 1968; Sandmo 1972; Dreze and Modigliani 1972; Zeldes 1989). The basic argument for the accumulation of assets by individuals can shed light on the accumulation of financial assets by the non-financial enterprise sectors in countries with exit-dominated financial systems.

Individuals who want to smooth consumption respond to uncertain fluctuations in earnings by accumulating savings to use as a buffer stock. I argue that one of the reasons that the non-financial enterprise sectors in countries with exit-dominated financial systems purchase more financial assets than the same sectors in countries with voice-dominated systems is to help smooth investment in the face of greater fluctuations in their sources of funds. The discussion in Chapter 4 demonstrated that the non-financial enterprise sectors in countries with exit-dominated financial systems face higher volatility of sources of funds than do those same sectors in countries with voice systems. Since sources of funds are equal to uses of funds, the volatility of uses of funds equals the volatility of sources of funds. Thus, countries with exit-dominated financial systems have more volatile uses of funds. For our purposes here, uses of funds can be decomposed into investment and financial asset purchases. Recalling the formula for the variance of the sum of two variables discussed earlier with respect to the sources side, the variance of uses of funds is, by definition, equal to the variance of investment plus the variance of financial asset purchases plus twice the covariance of investment and financial asset purchases:

$$\text{Var}(Uses) = \text{Var}(I) + \text{Var}(FAP) + 2\text{Cov}(I,FAP) \qquad (5.1)$$

In the next section, I will show that investment has been more variable in countries with exit-dominated financial systems. The argument presented in this chapter is that it would be even more variable were it not for the role of financial asset purchases as a buffer. The non-financial enterprise sectors in the US and UK have a greater variability in sources (uses) of funds. I argue that, in order to help smooth the variability of investment, these sectors invest less and vary to a greater extent their purchase of financial assets than do the same sectors in countries with voice systems. This is the precautionary motive for the purchase of financial assets: varying their purchase helps smooth investment in the face of greater variability of sources of funds. The greater variability in financial asset purchases is exhibited by the variability of the most liquid component of these financial asset purchases, bank deposits. The flows of bank deposits in the exit-dominated financial systems of the US and UK are between three and four times more volatile than those of the voice-dominated systems. The standard deviation of the growth rate of bank deposits over the period from 1970 to 1994 was 0.64 for Japan, 0.84 for Germany, 0.88 for France, 2.1 for the US, and 2.2 for the UK. These more volatile flows of bank deposits serve as a buffer to allow investment to vary less than sources of funds.

The non-financial enterprise sectors in the US and UK also purchase large amounts of equities. The purchase of these financial assets may be motivated by speculation and corporate control rather than the desire for a precautionary buffer against fluctuations in sources of funds. The speculative motive for purchasing an asset involves the purchase of that asset in the hope that the price of that asset will increase over the period for which the asset is held before it is sold. The speculative motive for purchasing shares has been associated with the reshuffling of corporate balance sheets associated with mergers, takeovers, buyouts, and stock repurchase programmes that have occurred in the US and UK since the early 1980s (Crotty and Goldstein 1993; Pollin 1994; Lee 1996). All of these activities involve the removal of equity from corporate balance sheets and are also likely to involve an increase in debt to finance the equity purchases. This removal, and its difference across financial system types, is evident when the amount of equity purchases as a share of total uses of funds over the period from 1970 to 1994 is examined. Equity purchases as a share of total uses of funds over this period was 12.7 per cent in the UK, 11.3 per cent in the US, 9.1 per cent in France, 2.8 per cent in Germany, and 0.8 per cent in Japan. The countries with exit-dominated financial systems purchased significantly more equities than did those with voice-dominated systems. This is true with the exception of France, which is an in-between case. Consistent with the evidence on convergence in the previous chapter, here again France lies between the two types of systems and is converging toward the exit model. The convergence of France toward the exit model will be a common theme of this chapter. With respect to the share of total uses of funds going to equity purchases, France's convergences can be seen by splitting the period into two time periods. From 1970 to 1983, the share of total uses going toward the purchase of equities was 2.8 per cent while the same ratio over the period from 1984 to 1994 was 16.5 per cent. There has been a significant increase in the purchase of equities in France's non-financial enterprise sector.

THE VOLATILITY OF INVESTMENT

The model developed in Chapter 3 suggests that the lower levels of borrower's and lender's risk in voice-dominated systems yield greater availability of external finance. This greater access to external finance allows underlying fluctuations of internal finance to be dampened and investment to be smoothed in voice-dominated systems while bank finance may exacerbate the volatility of internal finance in exit-dominated systems. The model thus suggests that investment will be more volatile in exit-dominated systems that rely more heavily on internal finance to fund investment and where bank finance is more volatile.

Evidence on the volatility of investment across countries is consistent with this prediction. Time series of quarterly real private gross fixed capital formation were constructed from *OECD Quarterly National Accounts*. Four-quarter growth rates were calculated from 1970 to 1994 to provide a measure of investment behaviour that could be readily compared across the five countries in question. The new growth rate series is calculated as follows:

$$i^k_t = (I^k_t - I^k_{t-4})/I^k_{t-4} \qquad (5.2)$$

where i refers to the growth rate and I refers to the level of investment in country k and the subscripts are quarterly time indexes.

To compare the variability of investment across these countries, a measure of investment volatility was obtained by calculating the standard deviation of the four-quarter investment growth rates over the whole period. This is measured as follows:

$$\sigma(i^t_k...i^T_k) \qquad (5.3)$$

These measures of investment volatility are displayed in Table 5.3. By this measure of investment volatility, investment is most volatile over this period in the US followed by the UK, Japan, Germany and France. The exit-dominated financial systems of the US and UK are associated with higher investment volatility than that of the voice-dominated systems. This ranking of countries by investment volatility is consistent with calculations of investment volatility found by Greenwald and Stiglitz (1988). By all measures of investment variability in their analysis, investment is most variable in the US followed by the UK, Germany and Japan.

Table 5.3: Investment volatility: 1970–1994

Country	Investment Volatility
Japan	0.0610
Germany	0.0560
France	0.0474
UK	0.0736
US	0.0823

Note: Investment volatility is measured by the standard deviation of four-quarter growth rates of real private gross fixed capital formation.

Source: Own calculations from *OECD Quarterly National Accounts*.

The exit-dominated financial systems of the US and UK are associated with greater investment volatility than the voice-dominated financial systems of France, Germany, and Japan. This is consistent with the model and the argument that the institutional arrangements for external financing in voice-dominated financial systems serve to help smooth investment. They help smooth investment by loosening the financial constraints on firms and allowing them greater access to external finance when internal finance falls than firms in exit-dominated financial systems.

INVESTMENT AND SOURCES OF FUNDS

Since internal funds are a large portion of total funds, it is possible that there is a tighter relationship between sources of funds and investment in voice-dominated systems simply because they invest a greater share of their funds. Time series plots of investment and total gross sources of funds for the non-financial enterprise sector of each country are shown in Figures 5.2 through 5.6. Exit-dominated systems purchase financial assets to a greater extent and these financial assets may, in part, serve as a buffer. When

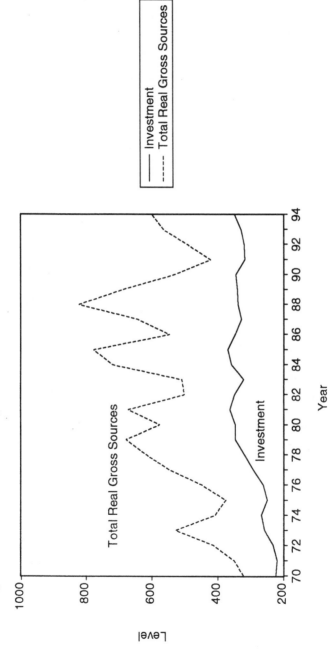

Figure 5.2 Investment and total real gross sources - US

Figure 5.3 Investment and total real gross sources - UK

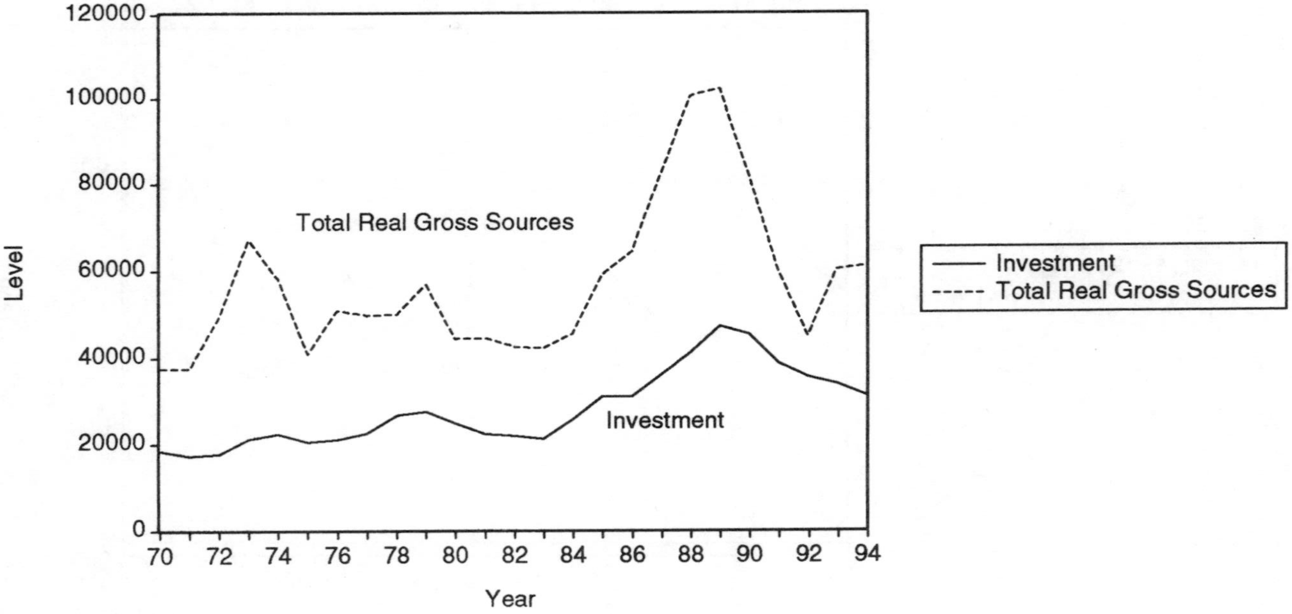

Figure 5.4 Investment and total real gross sources - Germany

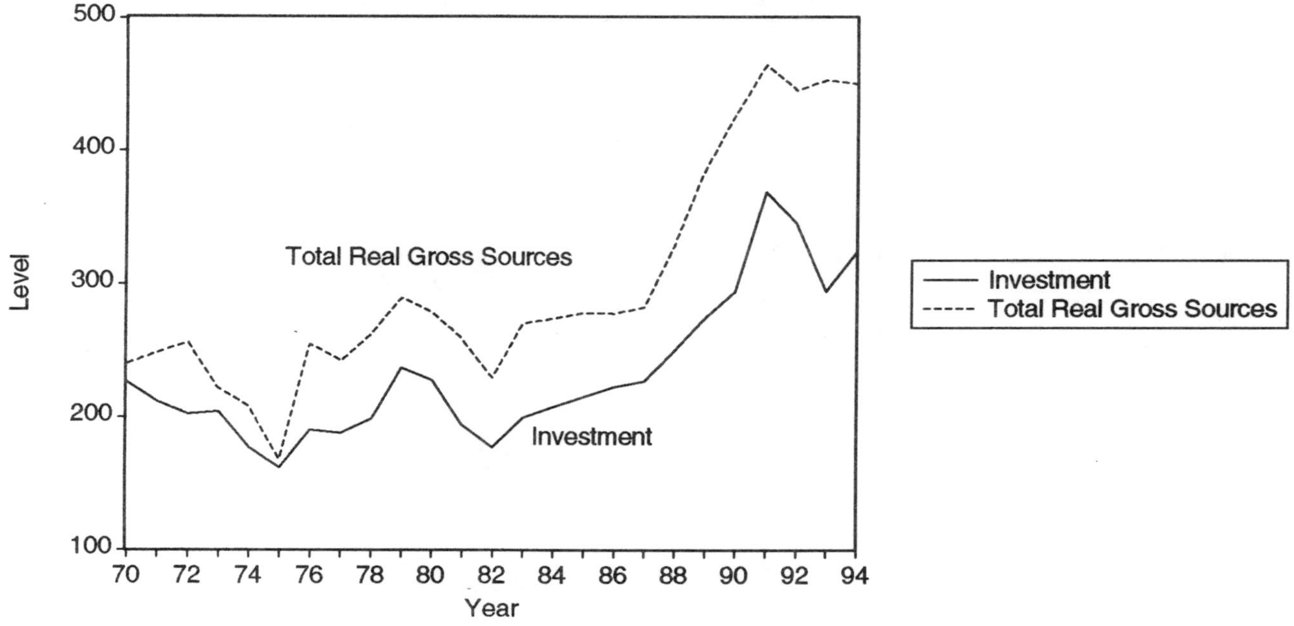

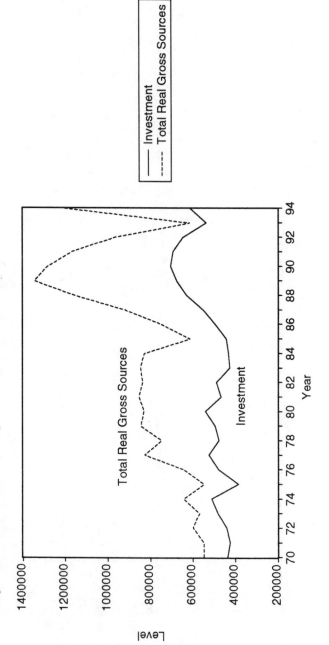

Figure 5.5 Investment and total real gross sources - France

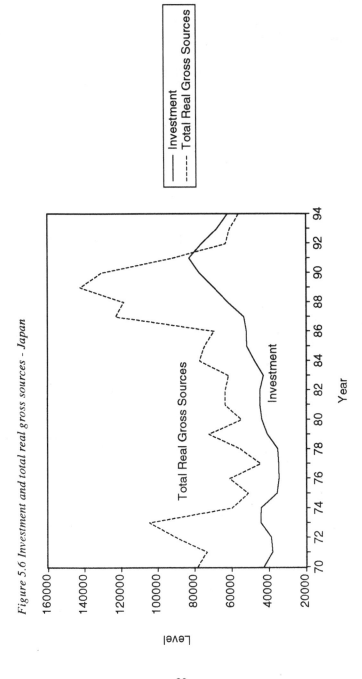

Figure 5.6 Investment and total real gross sources - Japan

sources of funds increase, exit-dominated financial systems may increase their purchase of financial assets and not real investment while voice-dominated financial systems do not respond to this increase in sources by purchasing financial assets but instead use these funds for investment. The relationship between investment and larger aggregates of sources of funds is investigated here.

In order to examine this possibility that investment might be more tightly linked to flows of finance in voice systems because of the propensity of exit-dominated systems to purchase financial assets rather than invest, regressions were run with investment regressed on the flow of total gross sources of funds and output. The regressions took the form:

$$I_t^k = C + b_1 TGS_t^k + b_2 Y_t^k \qquad (5.3)$$

where I_t^k is investment, C is a constant term, TGS_t^k is the flow of total gross sources of funds, and Y_t^k is output. Output is used as a control variable to try to discover whether the total flow of funds has a relationship to investment independent of changes in output.

The regression in equation 5.4 was run on the first differences of the series. If the coefficient on total gross sources were larger for voice-dominated system then that would indicate a tighter relationship between investment and total sources of funds. The results of these regressions are in Table 5.4.

Table 5.4: Regressions of investment on total gross sources of funds

Country	C	TGS	Y	R^2	D.W.
Japan	−2065	0.130	81750	0.603	1.732*
	(1559)	(0.036)**	(35856)*		
Germany	−10.4	0.332	547.3	0.510	2.286*
	(5.3)	(0.147)*	(198.3)*		
France	−39717	0.139	1804216	0.592	2.092*
	(14806)	(0.047)**	(552630)*		
US	−4.0	0.038	371.4	0.462	1.763*
	(4.3)	(0.034)	(148.4)*		
UK	−639	0.067	61515.8	0.489	1.580*
	(679)	(0.069)	(29721.7)*		

Notes:
a. Dependent variable is real investment.
b. All variables are in first differences and standard errors are in parentheses.
c. * indicates statistical significance at the 5 per cent level.
d. ** indicates significance at the 1 per cent level.

Neither of the exit-dominated systems display statistically significant coefficients on total gross sources. This indicates that there is no statistically significant relationship between investment and total sources of funds in exit systems. On the other hand, all of the voice-dominated financial systems have statistically significant positive coefficients on total gross sources. When the regression for France is split into two periods and one regression is run from 1970 to 1983 and another from 1984 to 1994, the coefficient on total gross sources is much higher in the earlier period than in the latter.[2] This is not surprising when Figure 5.5, the plot of investment and total gross sources in France, is examined, as there appears to be a break in the relationship in the early to mid-1980s. This is consistent with the evidence on convergence and, in particular, on the trend toward decreasing investment and increasing purchases of financial assets as a share of uses of funds presented in the previous chapter. Investment is less closely tied to total gross sources from 1984 to 1994 than it was previously. The relationship between investment and total sources of funds in France is becoming more like that found in the exit systems of the US and UK. Germany has the strongest relationship between investment and total sources of funds with a coefficient on total gross sources of 0.332. These regressions suggest that the total flow of financing has an independent impact on investment in voice-dominated financial systems when controlling for changes in output while there is no statistically significant relationship between investment and total gross sources of funds in the exit-dominated systems of the US and UK. This provides another distinguishing characteristic of financial systems that has not been discussed in the literature. Voice-dominated financial systems have a stronger relationship between the flow of sources of funds and investment than exit-dominated systems. This is consistent with the notion that exit-dominated systems invest less and vary their purchase of financial assets to buffer their more volatile flows of sources of funds and help smooth investment. Voice-dominated systems, in contrast, invest more, purchase fewer financial assets and rely on flows of external financing to help smooth investment.

To further test the relationship between investment and flows of financing across financial systems, the relationship between investment and a narrower measure of financing flows, ready funds, was examined. Plots of the time series of ready funds and investment for the five countries are shown in Figures 5.7 through 5.11. This measure was then used in a regression of investment on ready funds and output. The regression took the form:

$$I_t^k = C + b_1 RF_t^k + b_2 Y_t^k \qquad (5.4)$$

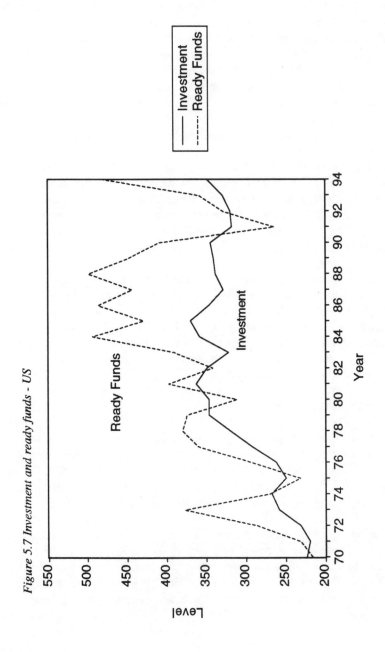

Figure 5.7 Investment and ready funds - US

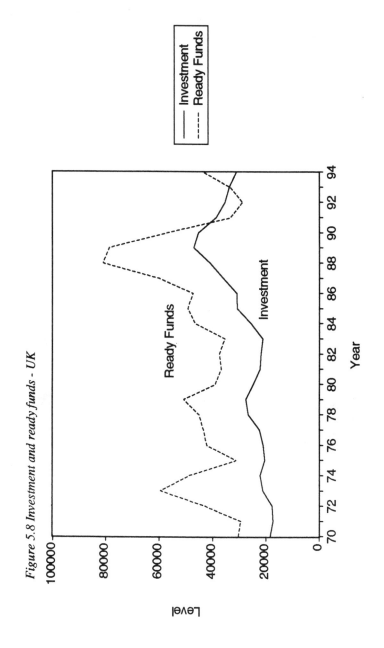

Figure 5.8 Investment and ready funds - UK

93

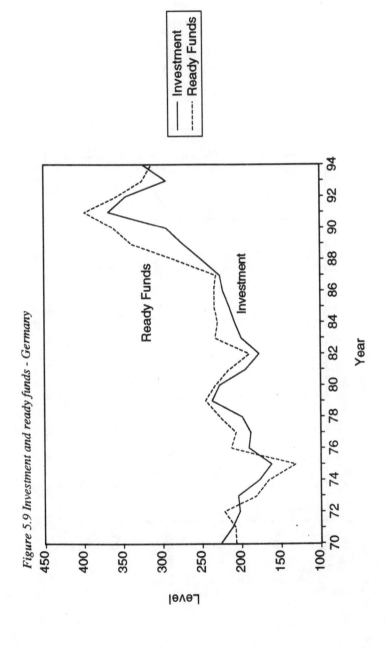

Figure 5.9 Investment and ready funds - Germany

94

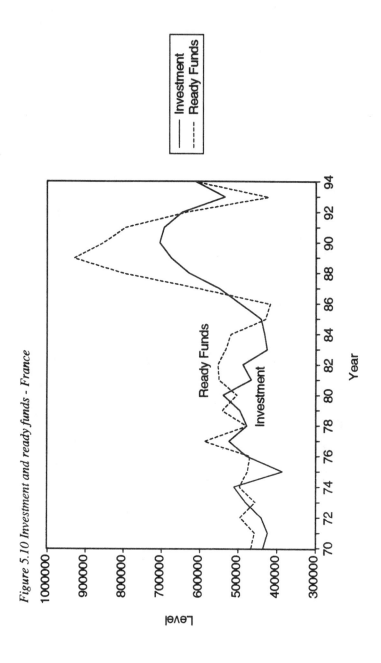

Figure 5.10 Investment and ready funds - France

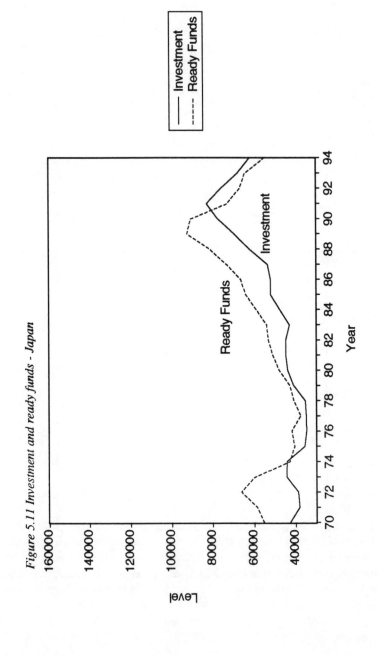

Figure 5.11 Investment and ready funds - Japan

where I_t^k is investment, C is an intercept term, RF_t^k is ready funds, and Y_t^k is logged output. The regression results of investment on ready funds and output are reported in Table 5.5.

Table 5.5: Regressions of investment on ready funds: 1970–1994

Country	C	RF	Y	R^2	D.W.
Japan	–2345	0.441	81989	0.708	1.633*
	(1273)	(0.088)**	(29614)*		
Germany	–7.99	0.400	490.17	0.563	2.134*
	(5.17)	(0.135)**	(188.79)*		
France	–41171	0.210	1972639	0.551	2.179*
	(15588)*	(0.085)*	(567315)**		
US	–5.42	0.035	433.9	0.441	1.782*
	(4.06)	(0.051)	(134.3)**		
UK	–780.1	0.042	71804	0.476	1.574*
	(675.1)	(0.066)	(27579)*		

Notes:
a. Dependent variable is real investment.
b. All variables are in first differences and standard errors are in parentheses.
c. * indicates statistical significance at the 5 per cent level.
d. ** indicates significance at the 1 per cent level.

The regression results indicate a statistically significant positive relationship between investment and ready funds in Japan, Germany, and France and no statistically significant relationship between these series in the US and UK. As discussed above for the regressions on total gross sources, the regression for France was split into two periods: from 1970 to 1983 and from 1984 to 1994. The coefficient on ready funds was significantly higher in the earlier period.[3] This is also consistent with the evidence presented in Chapter 2 regarding the increase in the purchase of financial assets and the decrease in investment as a share of uses of funds. A decreasing coefficient on ready funds is further evidence of the migration of France from a voice-dominated system to a system that more closely resembles the exit model. While keeping in mind the changes over time in France, there is a significant positive relationship between ready funds and investment while controlling for changes in output in voice-dominated financial systems. No such relationship exists in the exit-dominated systems. It has already been shown that ready funds are more volatile in exit-dominated systems because of the stronger positive relationship between internal funds and external funds. Exit-dominated systems cope with the lack of strong relationships between borrowers and lenders and the volatility in sources of funds by investing less in fixed assets and purchasing more financial assets to serve as a buffer for their more volatile flow of sources of funds to help smooth investment. The weak relationship between ready funds and investment for the exit-dominated systems is consistent with this notion. The relationship between investment and ready funds in voice-dominated systems is strong and ready funds are less volatile in these systems. This evidence supports the idea that these systems rely on flows of external finance to help smooth investment and do not purchase large amounts of financial assets. They rely on flows from lenders.

These results combined with the results of the examination of the relationship between the broader measure of total gross sources of funds and investment and the ratios of investment to total funds suggest that investment behaves differently across financial system types. Due to the fact that the exit-dominated financial systems purchase more financial assets and invest less out of their sources of funds, investment at the macro level may have a weaker relationship to measures of flows of funds. As was discussed in the earlier section on liquidity, this is likely to include internal funds. That is, internal funds and investment may have a weaker relationship at the macro level in exit-dominated systems.

INTERNAL FINANCE AND INVESTMENT

Quite a bit of evidence suggests that cash flow has an impact on investment in the US. The majority of this work has examined the relationship between cash flow and investment at the firm level. Fazzari and Mott (1986) find a significant independent effect of corporate cash flow on investment for manufacturing firms in the US once sales and other accelerator effects have been taken into account. Much of the evidence on the impact of cash flow on investment comes from firm panel data. Firms are split into two groups where one group would be expected to face greater financial constraints than the other. The more financially constrained firms are found to exhibit greater sensitivity of investment to cash flow. Fazzari, Hubbard, and Petersen (1988) made an early and important contribution. They classified US firms according to their dividend pay-out behaviour and found that investment by firms with a low pay-out ratio was more sensitive to cash flow in Q models of investment. Other evidence that cash flow has a greater impact on investment for firms facing greater financial constraints comes from work that splits the sample of firms according to other criteria.[4] One specific type of criteria used to split samples of firm panel data that is of interest here is membership in business groups that have close ties to banks. Results of studies that categorize firms according to membership in these groups show that there is less cash flow sensitivity for firms that are associated with a group.[5] Cross-country comparisons have also been made of the sensitivity of investment to cash flow at the firm level. Bond, Elston, Mairsse, and Mulkay (1995) conclude that the sensitivity of investment to cash flow is. greater for the UK than for France, Germany, or Belgium. Cummins, Hasset, and Hubbard (1994) find that cash flow coefficients are significant only for the US, UK, Norway, and Japan out of a set of 14 countries.

There have been, however, almost no studies of the relationship between investment and cash flow at the macro level or comparisons of this relationship across countries.[6] As discussed in the earlier section on liquidity, aggregating across firms will likely wash out most of the effect of financial constraints that some subsets of firms are experiencing. At the sectoral level, the relationship between flows of financing and investment will reflect how much of the flows of financing, on the margin, are going to investment. A tight relationship between investment and cash flow at the sectoral level does not indicate a financially constrained sector, although such a relationship at the firm level is taken as evidence of a financially constrained firm. A tight relationship at the sectoral level picks up the fact that much of the flows of financing are going toward investment.

To further investigate the relationship between investment and cash flow across financial systems, regressions were run between first differences of investment and first differences of lagged cash flow. The regressions took the form:

$$I_t^k = C + b_j CF_{t-1}^k \tag{5.6}$$

where I_t^k is the flow of investment for country k in year t, C is an intercept term and CF_t^k is the flow of internal finance in the prior period. The results of these regressions are in the Appendix. Considering these regressions, Germany, Japan, and France have larger coefficient values for the coefficient on cash flow than do the US and UK with all of the cash flow coefficients for the voice-dominated systems more than double that of the UK and nearly double that of the US. These results suggest that the voice-dominated financial systems have a tighter relationship between investment and cash flow than do the exit-dominated systems.

The cash flow variables could be simply picking up the impact of output on investment. To control for this and in order to further examine the relationship between internal funds and investment at a macro level, multivariate regressions were run between investment, cash flow, and both contemporaneous and lagged output. The regressions were of the form:

$$I_t^k = C + b_1 CF_{t-1}^k + b_2 Y_t^k + b_3 Y_{t-1}^k \qquad (5.7)$$

where I_t^k is investment in period t, C is an intercept term, CF_{t-1}^k is lagged cash flow, and Y_t and $b_3 Y_{t-1}^k$ are output and lagged output. If the coefficient on the cash flow variable is positive and significant while controlling for current and lagged output, then this would suggest an independent impact of cash flow on investment. The voice-dominated financial systems of Japan, and Germany have statistically significant positive coefficients on internal finance while the US and UK do not. This further indicates a tighter relationship between internal funds and investment in voice-dominated financial systems. The results of these regressions that control for changes in output for the most part echo the results of the bivariate regressions from equation 5.6. Unlike the bivariate regression, however, when controlling for current and lagged output, France does not have a statistically significant cash flow coefficient. The results of these regressions are reported in the Appendix.

CONCLUSION

How might the relationships between internal and external sources of funds and investment differ across financial systems? Chapters 4 and 5 provide new evidence on this question. Models of investment behaviour following Minsky (1975) have been concerned with the relationship between financial conditions and investment. Specifically, they have been concerned with how the level of borrower's risk and lender's risk impacts on investment. This literature has developed with the financial institutions of the United States as the implicit or explicit institutional context. Chapter 3 adapts the Minsky model to take into consideration that the level of borrower's risk and lender's risk may differ across financial systems. Borrower's risk and lender's risk have been explained as functions of leverage and claimed to vary over the business cycle. The adaptation of Chapter 3 suggests that these risks are not uniquely determined by leverage but that different institutional arrangements between borrowers and lenders in different financial systems may mitigate these risks. The adapted model suggested several propositions regarding the behaviour of, and the different relationships between, investment, cash flow, and external finance.

The relationship between external finance and internal finance across the five countries was empirically examined. The results first showed that bank finance was more volatile in exit systems while the volatility of internal funds was nearly identical across the countries in question. It was then shown that bank finance is more strongly positively related to internal finance in countries with exit-dominated financial systems. Bank finance is negatively related to internal funds in Germany, France, and Japan. This relationship, combined with the varying volatilities of bank finance, makes ready funds, an aggregate defined as the sum of internal funds and bank finance, more volatile in the exit-dominated financial systems of the US and UK. Bank finance plays more of a smoothing role in the voice-dominated systems by being less positively related – and sometimes negatively related to internal funds--in the countries with voice-dominated systems.

This lower volatility in sources of funds was argued to help the non-financial enterprise sector in the countries with voice-dominated financial systems achieve higher and less volatile investment. Investment was shown to have been higher in countries with voice-dominated systems at both the level of the economy as a whole and at the sectoral level from 1970 to 1994. The non-financial enterprise sectors of countries with exit-dominated financial systems invested less and purchased more financial assets as a share of total gross sources of funds than did the same sectors in countries with voice-dominated systems. These countries were also shown to have lower volatilities of investment over this period.

The fact that the non-financial enterprise sectors of countries with voice-dominated financial systems invested more of their gross sources of funds was demonstrated by time series regressions of investment on various aggregates of sources of financing in addition to whole-period averages. Investment was shown to be more closely related to flows of finance at the sectoral level in countries with voice-dominated financial systems. The investment regressions that regressed investment on flows of financing sources for the countries with voice-dominated financial systems had statistically significantly larger coefficients on all measures of flows of financing including internal finance.   More is invested out of each additional dollar of financing in the non-financial enterprise sector of countries with voice-dominated financial systems than in countries with exit-dominated systems. This provides another distinguishing characteristic of financial systems that has not been discussed in the literature. At the sectoral level, countries with voice-dominated financial systems have a stronger relationship between the flow of sources of funds and investment than do countries with exit-dominated financial systems.

Another important insight of these chapters is the evidence presented that suggests France is drifting toward the exit model. Chapter 2 discussed the convergence of France toward the exit-dominated systems of the US and UK when measured in terms of the pattern of sources and uses of funds. This chapter suggests that this convergence is also occurring in the relationship between, and behaviour of, investment and sources of funds. When the regressions of investment on flows of financing were split into two periods, France exhibited a considerable reduction in the coefficient on sources of funds in the latter period from 1984 to 1994. The non-financial enterprise sector in France invested less out of each Franc of financing in the latter period than it did in the earlier period. These regression results are consistent with the fact that, over time, the non-financial enterprise sector in France has begun to invest less and purchase more financial assets out of total sources of funds.

NOTES

1 For the period 1960-1992 Japan's investment (gross fixed capital formation and changes in stocks) averaged 33.5 per cent of GDP, France's averaged 24.1 per cent, and Germany's averaged 23.7 per cent while the US's averaged 19.1 per cent and the UK's averaged 18.4 per cent (calculations based on IMF 1993).

2 In the period from 1970 to 1983 the coefficient on total gross sources for France is 0.428 (s.e. 0.184) while in the period from 1984 to 1994 the coefficient on total gross sources is 0.099 (s.e. 0.041).

3 The coefficient on ready funds for the period from 1970 to 1983 is 0.466 (s.e. 0.352) and 0.194 (s.e. 0.090) for the period from 1984 to 1994.

4 Whited (1992) splits firms according to whether or not they have a bond rating. Devereux and Schiantarelli (1990) categorize firms by size and age. Calomaris, Himmelberg, and Wachtel (1995) categorize firms according to whether or not they possess a commercial paper rating.

5 Hoshi, Kashyap, and Scharfstein (1990) show that investment by Japanese firms with close ties to large banks was less sensitive to cash flow than in another group of Japanese firms without strong links to a main bank. Evidence is also available at the firm level for Italy (Schiantarelli and Sembenelli 1995), Korea (Cho 1995), Germany (Elston and Albach 1995), and Canada (Schaller 1993).

6 Jacobs (1994) finds investment is less sensitive to the profit rate in countries with bank-based systems, but this is quite different from cash flow. Mahdavi, Sohrabian, and Kholdy (1994) find that in the US, cash flow and investment are cointegrated and that, using error correction models, investment Granger causes cash flow using quarterly data at the macro-level.

APPENDIX

Table A5.1: Investment – cash flow regressions: 1970–1994[a]

Country	C	CF	R^2	D.W.
Germany	2.239	0.715	0.231	2.317*
	(5.031)	(0.259)**		
Japan	400.2	0.643	0.160	0.830
	(984.1)	(0.282)*		
Japan AR(1)[b]	−595.7	0.720	0.402	1.586*
	(2208.6)	(0.267)*		
France	508.5	0.586	0.086	2.510
	(12658)	(0.335)		
France AR(1)[c]	-2802	0.730	0.144	2.157*
	(9694)	(0.291)*		
US	2.076	0.389	0.163	2.032*
	(3.940)	(0.170)*		
UK	382.2	0.295	0.166	1.358*
	(645.4)	(0.127)*		

Notes:
a Dependent variable is real gross private investment and cash flow variable is lagged one period. All variables are in first differences and standard errors are in parenthesis. * indicates statistical significance at the 5 per cent level and ** indicates significance at the 1 per cent level.
b. An AR(1) correction was made for the Japan regression to correct for the presence of positive serial correlation.
c. An AR(1) correction was made for the regression for France to correct for the presence of negative serial correlation.

Table A5.2: Regressions of investment on cash flow and output

Country	C	CF$_{-1}$	Y	Y$_{-1}$	R^2	D.W.
Japan	−6173.7**	0.415*	106373*	73927*	0.622	1.414*
	(1480.5)	(0.206)	(29469)	(35846)		
Germany	−6.212	0.443*	754.9**	−287.8	0.555	2.322*
	(5.742)	(0.210)	(183.2)	(173.0)		
France	−45174*	0.155	3082955**	−806717	0.558	2.283*
	(17770)	(0.254)	(623829)	(554279)		
US	−9.72*	0.142	417.6**	145.7	0.564	1.536*
	(3.94)	(0.127)	(102.8)	(104.5)		
UK	−1702**	−0.015	72042**	54176*	0.646	2.014*
	(5850	(0.115)	(15719)	(21054)		

Notes: Dependent variable is real gross bank finance. All variables are in first differences and standard errors are in parenthesis. * Indicates statistical significance at the 5 per cent level and ** indicates statistical significance at the 1 per cent level.

6. Globalization and the Convergence of National Financial Systems

GLOBALIZATION OF FINANCIAL MARKETS

Financial markets are becoming increasingly globalized. There are at least three separable approaches to measuring the global integration of financial markets: the legal, quantity, and price approaches (Cosh, Hughes and Singh 1992). The legal approach examines to what degree the law allows for various types of cross-border financial flows while the quantity approach measures the volume of such flow. The price approach attempts to measure the internationalization of a market by the degree to which it obeys the law of one price.

The legal approach to globalization requires an examination of changes in financial market regulations across countries. One possible understanding of globalization is that it is the process of creating, or tendency toward, a single global financial market. This is a process of integration of different national financial markets into a homogeneous global market. In order to achieve this homogeneity, differences in national financial markets must be minimized. Differences in financial markets are often due to differences in regulations regarding their operation. Deregulation of national financial markets that seek to harmonize regulations with those of other nations is thus an important aspect of the globalization process.

The practices of 'regulatory arbitrage' or 'regulatory whipsawing' that seek to remove regulations on financial market activity are part of the liberalization of financial markets that has constituted the process of creating a global financial market (Cerny 1994; Herring and Litan 1995). This is a competition in laxity whereby countries remove regulations in order to prevent the perceived threat or actual movement of financial activity abroad. This widespread removal of financial market regulations and the arguments to do so mark the move from the devotion to viewing the world economy via a Keynesian or 'national' model to what has been called 'global neoclassicism' (Schor 1992).   This latter view argues that international financial regulation is futile and that governments should not control cross-border capital flows or pursue regulations or policies which are different from those dictated by global markets. I concur and argue that a rethinking of the types of regulations and policy tools dealing with the real changes that have taken place in financial markets partly as a result of their globalization is sorely needed. It is exactly this type of policy and regulatory response that is explored in Chapter 7 of this book.

   A major thrust of the liberalization trend that has allowed globalization to take place is the removal of capital controls. Capital controls restrict the ability of agents to conduct foreign exchange transactions and may prohibit certain types of foreign exchange transactions entirely. After years of restricted capital flows (Hawley 1987), restrictions on capital flows were removed in 1974 in the US. They were removed in 1979 in the UK and Japan (Epstein and Schor 1992). Capital controls were removed in France in 1984 as part of a much larger reform of the nation's financial system (Melitz 1990). In the same year the OECD began to overhaul its 'Codes of Liberalisation of Capital Movements and Current Invisible Operations' and liberalized direct investments. In 1989, the codes were amended to cover the banking and financial services sectors (Ley 1989).[1]   The removal of these controls allowed foreign currency investments. This increased the potential substitutability of domestic and foreign assets. It also opened up the possibility of firms accessing markets around the world in search of the best financing terms. Firms with global operations can obtain financing from major money centres across the globe (Resnick 1989).   On this point, Inoue claims that the sources of funds to Japanese enterprises through capital markets have been substantially globalized (Inoue 1989, p.57).

   In addition to capital controls, liberalization has touched many other areas of financial markets. Regulations that compartmentalized financial institutions, limiting them to particular practices, have been removed in France. Limits on interest rates as well as quantity restrictions have been eliminated in both Japan and France. Rules pertaining to equity markets have been relaxed and markets in various types of securities have been allowed to develop where they were previously prohibited in Germany, France, and Japan. All of these changes are part of the liberalization dynamic that is a major feature of the globalization process. This dynamic has, as will be discussed at greater length later, caused structural changes in countries' financial systems that have led to the loss of direct controls over the supply and allocation of credit that monetary authorities previously had at their disposal.

The creation and growth of the Euromarkets is another important component of the globalization process. These markets are credit and capital markets that are denominated in currencies other than that of the country in which the market is located (e.g. a dollar denominated bond sold in France or a dollar denominated loan made in the UK). These markets arose in response to earlier attempts to restrict capital flows and regulate financial markets. The Euromarkets have a competitive advantage over domestic markets because Eurocurrency deposits face no reserve requirements, pay for no deposit insurance, have no interest rate regulations, and pay low or no taxes. In addition, Eurobonds are virtually unregulated and can be brought to market more quickly and at a lower cost than domestic bonds (Resnick 1989, p.36; Sarver 1990). Their presence has both helped to force the liberalization of national markets and served as a significant step in the process of creating a global financial market.

Growth of these markets helped create pressure for countries to liberalize as in the initiation of International Banking Facilities (IBF's) in the US.[2] The market for loans from these deposits, as well as for Eurobonds, created a source of funds that could be tapped by certain classes of borrowers around the globe and served as a pressure point for liberalization. The Euromarkets provided a rupture of the connection between financial markets and national regulation: they were offshore markets that did not fall within the jurisdiction of any country. In that sense, they marked the creation of a global market outside the context of any national financial system.

QUANTITY MEASURES OF INTEGRATION

These changes and the removal of capital controls there has led to a rapid increase in cross border financial flows. Although no comprehensive measure of gross international financial flows exists, there are several indicators that show their growth. One proxy is the volume of payments cleared through the Clearing House Interbank Payment System (CHIPS), the computerized payment system that processes international transactions based on US dollars. By 1993 the average daily volume of transactions cleared on this system was over $1 trillion which is up almost sevenfold from the 1980 level of transactions (Herring and Litan 1995, p. 24). Simultaneously, the stock of international bank loans nearly quadrupled in the 1980s. While the stock of bank loans is still larger than the stock of international bonds, the flow of new bond issues has been higher than that of new loans since 1983 (*OECD Financial Market Trends*, February 1993, pp. 6, 117).

PRICE MEASURES OF INTEGRATION

As financial markets become increasingly globalized, arbitrage should drive the risk-adjusted rate of return on similar financial assets into uniformity. That is, the process of globalization should make it easier for the law of one price to hold for like assets. There are four price measures used to gauge the degree of international financial market integration by examining the behaviour of interest rates on assets denominated in different currencies or held across borders: closed interest rate parity, covered interest rate parity, uncovered interest rate parity, and real interest rate parity.[3]

Closed Interest Rate Parity

Closed interest rate parity is achieved when interest rates on comparable financial instruments denominated in the same currency but issued in different countries are the same. Capital controls of various kinds can drive a wedge between the rates of return available on like assets denominated in the same currency but located in different countries. The removal of capital controls in almost all industrialized countries and the increase in cross border financial flows has allowed arbitrage to force closed interest parity to hold.[4] Offshore and onshore markets of the major industrialized countries for assets denominated in the same currency are nearly fully integrated, if judged by the closed interest rate parity condition.

Covered Interest Rate Parity

The condition for covered interest rate parity is satisfied when the rates of return on like assets denominated in different currencies are equal after allowing for the cost of covering the currency risk with a forward currency contract. The covered interest rate parity condition can be expressed as

$$i_{mt} - i^*_{mt} = Fd_m \qquad (6.1)$$

where i_{mt} is the domestic interest rate at time t on an asset with m periods to maturity, i^*_{mt} is the foreign rate and Fd_m is the foreign discount (premium). For the major industrial economies and a growing number of other countries, covered interest rate parity holds (Herring and Litan 1995).[5]

Uncovered Interest Rate Parity

For uncovered interest rate parity to hold, nominal interest rate differentials between assets denominated in two currencies have to equal the expected change in the exchange rate over the period to maturity for these assets. This condition can be expressed as

$$i_{mt} - i^*_{mt} = E[\Delta(S_{mt})] \tag{6.2}$$

where $E[\Delta(S_{mt})]$ is the expected change in the exchange rate and the left hand side the difference between the domestic and foreign rates on assets with m periods to maturity at time t. If covered interest rate parity holds, then tests for condition (6.2) have embedded in them the tests for the degree to which forward rates are unbiased predictors of future spot exchange rates. This can be seen by combining (6.1) and (6.2) to get

$$Fd_m = E[\Delta(S_{mt})] \tag{6.3}$$

A large number of studies have found that this condition does not hold; that is, the forward exchange rate premia is not an unbiased predictor of future changes in spot foreign exchange rates.[6] Two explanations of the standard rejection of uncovered interest rate parity in regression tests, McCallum's (1994) and Frankel and Froot's (1990), are consistent with uncovered interest rate parity.[7]

Real Interest Rate Parity

The condition for real interest rate parity can be found by combining (6.2), the condition for uncovered parity, with the following condition for ex ante purchasing power parity

$$E[\Delta(S_{mt})]=E(\Pi_{mt}) - E(\Pi^*_{mt}) \tag{6.4}$$

that says the expected change in the nominal exchange rate over m periods is equal to the difference between the domestic expected inflation rate over m periods and the foreign expected inflation rate over the same period of time. Combining uncovered interest parity (6.2) with ex ante purchasing power parity (6.4) we get the condition for real interest parity

$$i_{mt} - E(\Pi_{mt})= i^*_{mt} - E(\Pi^*_{mt}) \tag{6.5}$$
$$\text{or}$$
$$E(r_{mt})=E(r^*_{mt}) \tag{6.6}$$

which says that domestic ex ante real interest rates are equal to foreign ex ante real interest rates. Testing this condition is difficult because ex ante interest rates are not observable. Real interest parity has been rejected in the majority of econometric tests.[8] The rejection of real interest rate parity does not mean that financial markets are not integrated. If financial markets are integrated in the sense of uncovered interest rate parity being satisfied but goods markets are not fully integrated, that is, with purchasing power parity failing to hold, then tests for real interest parity would fail. The failure of real interest rate parity is consistent with both the integration of financial markets and the ability of domestic monetary authorities to have independent effects on interest rates.[9] With flexible exchange rates and distinct economic conditions in different countries, interest rate differentials across countries should be expected even with 'perfect' capital mobility and financial integration.

The process of globalization of financial markets has produced fairly well integrated global markets for a wide class of financial assets. Once there is agreement that financial markets in the industrial countries are fairly well integrated, a question to be addressed is does this degree of financial market integration mark an historically unique circumstance?

IS THE PRESENT PERIOD OF FINANCIAL MARKET INTEGRATION HISTORICALLY UNIQUE?

While acknowledging a growing openness in financial markets since World War II, some authors, like Zevin (1992), examine price correlations and conclude that there does not exist a single integrated market. Their argument is that the level of integration is neither dramatic nor unique when considered over a longer span of history.[10] However, focusing only on price correlations does not address the notion that financial markets are larger and more complex than they were previously and that this provides a much different context for the growing integration of financial markets. With more complex and overlapping financial arrangements, open and integrated financial markets may create greater financial fragility and instability now than in prior periods when a smaller number of asset markets were integrated. This possibility is not considered by those who are interested only in the degree of financial integration as measured by the correlation of asset prices across countries.

Another aspect of the missing context in focusing exclusively on price tests is the development of national Keynesian macroeconomic policies that did not exist in earlier periods of high capital mobility. Taking this into account, financial market integration now is different from that of previous periods because of its impact on macroeconomic policies that were not in existence during these earlier periods of high financial integration. For example, financial markets in eighteenth-century Western Europe, for those few assets that existed, were fairly well integrated but this integration had no effect on monetary policy because monetary policy, such as it was, was not geared toward domestic economic management.

Financial markets could be equally integrated in two periods on the basis of asset price correlation with very different effects (e.g., on macroeconomic policy and financial fragility). Thus, if the growth in global bond markets and increasing integration have reduced monetary authorities' abilities to control long-term rates, then financial integration now differs from earlier periods when the ability to conduct effective monetary policy was not an issue. In order to investigate how globalization as a process has affected national financial systems and the conduct of monetary policy, these other dimensions need to be explored.

GLOBALIZATION AND THE CONVERGENCE OF NATIONAL FINANCIAL SYSTEMS

A major point of emphasis in the more recent literature on national financial systems is the argument that as financial markets become increasingly international in character and as financial liberalization programmes proceed, a convergence of national financial systems will occur. Moran (1991) writes that although the banking and securities industries have developed different institutional arrangements in different countries, what he terms the financial services revolution 'consists of a growing similarity between the institutional structures and trading practices in the financial markets of all the major capitalist economies' (p. 9). National financial systems are said to be converging toward the 'Anglo-Saxon' or market-based model.

Bank-based systems are described as 'uncompetitive' in this new era of globalization of financial markets (Capoglu 1994). Are these systems uncompetitive, losing their institutional distinctiveness and converging toward the capital market-based model? A brief review of the literature on this point will help answer this question. Rybczynski suggests that 'while there are at present marked differences between bank-oriented financial systems on the Continent of Europe and Japan on the one hand and market-oriented systems in the UK and a strongly market-oriented system in the US, strong forces have been at work in recent years working toward slow convergence' (1984, p. 282). Berglöf, pointing out the same trend, argues that 'due to recent developments in the financial markets, in particular increasing securitization and internationalization, financial systems have converged along some dimensions' (1989, p.245). Jensen claims 'there is some evidence that the national systems are converging--that Japan and Germany are moving toward a more American-like system' (1991, p.75).

With regard to national financial structures, Cumming and Sweet note that while 'individual country approaches often reflect unique historical factors, yet broad international developments have increasingly influenced the financial systems of most nations' (1988, p.14). Gardener and Molyneux claim that 'globalization trends are rendering traditional national sovereignty in financial systems an anachronism' (1990, p.1). They claim that specialization and national control of financial systems were important parts of twentieth century banking but that internationalization and technological changes are creating greater homogeneity among the financing possibilities facing large multinational corporations. Gardener and Molyneux do, however, believe that significant country differences still persist (p.112). Henning (1994, pp. 48-58) cites evidence of recent convergence among the financial structures of Germany, Japan, and the US arguing that Japan has changed more than the others although the fundamental differences between the two types of systems still remain. Frankel and Montgomery (1991, pp.257-8) note the recent changes in the financial structures of many countries but discount the emergence of a single model.[11]   Cosh, Hughes and Singh (1992) predict that the relationship between financial and industrial capital will become more short term, more 'arm's length' and more diffuse.

As noted above, there are many references in the literature to changes in financial systems.   There has been, however, very little empirical work and no formal econometric work on the subject.[12]   The question addressed here is whether or not there has been a convergence of national financial systems as a result of the globalization process taking place in financial markets.   Are there still significant differences in financial systems or have the changes in financial markets eroded the differences? This question is addressed by examining how the patterns of financing in both exit- and voice-dominated financial systems have changed over time by constructing time series of both the sources and uses of financing. In addition to providing descriptive statistics as to how these patterns have changed over time, the book provides econometric examinations of the time series on sources and uses of financing from 1970 to 1994 in order to examine the convergence claim.

CONVERGENCE

As noted above, there are many references in the literature to changes in financial systems. There has been, however, little investigation of the changing structure of national financial systems. Corbett and Jenkinson (1996), offer the only direct multi-country examination of the convergence claim that examines changes in the pattern of sources of industrial finance over time. However, Bertero (1994) offers a useful examination of changes in the French financial system over time with an interest in the question of convergence. The question to be addressed here is whether or not there has been a convergence of national financial systems as a result of the globalization process taking place in financial markets. Are voice-dominated systems still clearly different from exit-dominated systems, or have the changes in financial markets eroded the differences?

Measuring for Convergence

Time series of sources of financing are calculated for five countries: the US, UK, France, Germany, and Japan. This is done in order to investigate the question of the convergence of these financial systems. By comparing the patterns of financing sources and uses of funds for these countries, we can discover whether the patterns of financing sources and uses by non-financial enterprises in these countries have become more similar. Specifically, I want to answer the question of whether the voice-dominated systems of Japan, Germany, and France have become, by these measures, more like the exit-dominated systems of the US and UK.

Overall, the changing patterns of financing across the countries examined in Chapter 2 suggest that Japan, and especially France, have recently shown convergence toward the internally financed exit model of the US and the UK. Germany has not shown a similar convergence. This section further examines the evidence on convergence.

Sources

To test for the possibility of a convergence with respect to the shares of different types of financing, new series consisting of the standard deviations of each group of series were calculated over the period 1970–1995. For example, for the group of series on internal funds as a share of total gross sources of funds for each of the countries, the standard deviation series s_t^{GIF} is calculated as:

$$s_t^{GIF} = \sigma_t(GIF_t^J, \, GIF_t^G, \, GIF_t^F, \, GIF_t^{US}, \, GIF_t^{UK}) \qquad (6.7)$$

where GIF_t^i is the share of internal funds in total gross sources in year t for country i. If the standard deviation exhibits a negative trend, this would indicate a tighter dispersion of these values over time. In order to test formally for the presence of trends in the standard deviation series, regressions were run of the form:

$$s_t^i = C + b_l T \qquad (6.8)$$

where s_t^i is the standard deviation in year t for financing source i for the group of countries as calculated above, C is a constant term, and T is a time trend variable. A negative coefficient on the time trend would indicate a negative trend for the standard deviation. This would indicate a tightening dispersion of the shares of financing of type i and would be evidence of convergence for the group of countries as a whole. The results of these regressions for gross and net bank finance and internal finance are reported in Table 6.1.

Table 6.1: Time trend regressions – standard deviations of net and gross internal and bank finance for the five countries: 1970–1995

Financing	Share of Gross Sources			Share of Net Sources		
	C	b_l	R^2	C	b_l	R^2
Internal	0.115	–0.0004	–0.031	0.159	–0.0008	-0.016
	(0.012)	(0.0008)		(0.016)	(0.0011)	
Bank	0.100	0.0001	–0.041	0.095	0.0022	0.060
	(0.016)	(0.0011)		(0.020)	(0.0014)	

Notes:
a. Dependent variable is the standard deviation of either internal funds or bank finance as a share of total gross sources or as a share of total net sources for the group of five countries.
b. Standard errors are in parentheses.
c. * indicates statistical significance at the 5 per cent level.
d. ** indicates significance at the 1 per cent level.

None of these regressions show evidence of a convergence of the five countries' shares of internal funds or bank finance on either a gross or net basis. Tests for the presence of unit roots in these series confirmed the results of the time trend regressions.[13] Thus, there is no evidence of convergence based on an examination of these for the group as a whole. It is, however, possible that one or more of the voice-dominated financial systems is converging toward the exit model while others are not. This would be masked by the group standard deviation calculations. In order to examine this possibility each country must first be examined individually and then compared to an exit model benchmark to check for cases of individual financial system convergence.

As a further test of whether or not the financial systems of Germany, France, and Japan are converging toward the exit model, time series of bank finance and internal funds on both a gross and net basis were tested for time trends. For each of the countries, regressions were run in which the series in question, either net or gross bank finance or internal funds, was regressed against a time trend. A statistically significant positive (negative) coefficient on the time trend term would indicate a positive (negative) trend. For the voice-dominated financial systems of Germany, France, and Japan, a necessary condition of their convergence toward the exit model of the US and UK would be a positive trend in the share of internal funds in total sources of funds and a negative trend in the share of bank finance.

For the series on internal funds, regressions took the form:

$$IF_t^i = C + b_1T \qquad (6.9)$$

Where IF_t^i is the share of internal funds in total net or gross sources in country i in year t, C is a constant term and T is a time trend variable. The regression results with respect to internal funds are shown in the Appendix to this chapter. These results indicate that France and Japan have statistically significant positive trends for the share of internal funds in both the net and gross sources. For Germany, the share of internal funds in net and gross sources of funds shows no statistically significant trend in either case. The same is true for the UK while the share of internal funds in the US shows a positive trend for both the gross and net shares series. This fulfils one of the necessary conditions for the convergence of the French and Japanese financial systems: internal finance is becoming increasingly important. They are, however, converging toward a bit of a moving target as the US system continues to increase its reliance on internal funds while the UK does not. Germany does not exhibit the convergence on the basis of reliance upon internal funds that we see in the cases of France and Japan.

The regressions for bank finance were of the form:

$$BF_t^i = C + b_1T \qquad (6.10)$$

where BF_t^i is either the share in total gross or net sources of funds of gross or net flows of bank finance in year t in country i, C is an intercept term, and T is a time trend variable. The regression results with respect to bank finance support the claim that Japan and France have experienced considerable convergence toward the exit-dominated financial systems of the US and UK. Bank finance in both Japan and France, on both a net and gross basis, has shown a statistically significant negative trend over the past twenty-five years. As in the case of internal funds, Germany exhibits no convergence toward the exit model when bank finance is examined.

The above analysis suggests that France and Japan are increasing their use of internal sources of funds and decreasing their use of bank finance. This is preliminary evidence of convergence for these two financial systems. To further examine this convergence, one needs to analyse how close these trends have moved the financial systems of France and Japan to the pattern of financing exhibited in the exit systems of the US and UK. Toward this end, an exit model benchmark was created by creating series that averaged the shares of internal funds and bank finance used in the US and UK. These new series were then fitted with linear trends. These trends are then defined as the exit model benchmark against which movements in the shares of internal funds and bank finance in France, Japan, and Germany will be compared.

To make this comparison, deviations from the exit model trend values were calculated for each country. These deviations were calculated as simple differences. The calculations for deviations in internal funds from the exit model trend in country i were made as follows:

$$IFDEV_t^i = (IF_t^{exit} - IF_t^i) \qquad (6.11)$$

where $IFDEV_t^i$ is the deviation from the exit model trend for country i in year t, IF_t^{exit} is the exit model trend value in year t for the share of internal funds, and IF_t^i is the share of internal funds in year t in country i. The deviations for bank finance were calculated in a similar fashion. The only difference is that the share of bank finance for the exit model trend is subtracted from the share of bank finance in the country in question. For bank finance the calculations are as follows:

$$BFDEV_t^i = (BF_t^i - BF_t^{exit}) \qquad (6.12)$$

This is done for ease of comparison to ensure positive deviations, as is the case with internal funds, because the shares of bank finance in the exit model are lower than those in Germany, France, and Japan. If these deviations are decreasing over time, then that is evidence of convergence in the use of internal funds and bank finance toward the exit model for the country in question.

The deviations for shares of net internal funds are shown for France, Japan, and Germany in Figures 6.1, 6.2, and 6.3, respectively. France clearly shows decreasing deviations from the exit model trend for the share of internal funds in total net sources. The convergence begins in the early 1980s and by the early 1990s, France's net share of internal funds is higher than that of the exit model trend. Japan's convergence begins later than that of France. This can be seen in Figure 6.2 which shows a steady fall in Japan's deviation from the exit model trend beginning in 1990. By 1994, Japan's share of internal funds in total net sources was equal to that of the exit model trend. Germany shows no such convergence, as can be seen in Figure 6.3. In fact, in the 1990s, Germany has shown larger deviations from the exit model trend than at any prior point.

The deviations for shares of internal funds in total gross sources for France, Japan, and Germany were also examined.[14] France and Japan show a recent negative trend and thus a convergence toward the exit model. France diverges from the exit model benchmark from 1970 until the early 1980s and then converges for the remainder of the period. Germany displays no such movement.

In order to test for the presence of statistically significant time trends in these deviations that would indicate convergence, the deviations of internal funds from the exit model were regressed against time trend variables. This was done on both a gross and net basis for France, Japan, and Germany. The regressions were of the form:

$$IFDEV_t^i = C + b_i T \qquad (6.13)$$

The results of these regressions are reported in Table 6.2. The regression results confirm what the plots suggested. France and Japan have statistically significant negative trends for both the net and gross deviations while Germany has no statistically significant trend for either series. In order to test further these series for the presence of trends, stationarity tests were run on all six of the series. The results of these tests confirm the results from the trend regressions.[15] This is evidence of convergence for France and Japan with respect to their use of internal funds. Germany has not converged along this dimension.

Figures 6.4, 6.5, and 6.6 show the time series plots of the deviations of the shares of net bank finance in total net sources from the exit model for France, Japan, and Germany. These plots show trends similar to those of the plots of the gross share deviations. France and Japan show negative trends while Germany does not. The deviations with respect to the shares of gross bank finance in total gross sources support the same patterns of convergence: France and Japan converge while Germany does not. The deviations for France show a negative trend and a convergence toward the exit model. The same is true for Japan. Germany shows no convergence over time toward the exit model, although in the earlier part of the period Germany shows smaller deviations from the exit model than Japan or France. There is no negative trend in Germany's deviations.

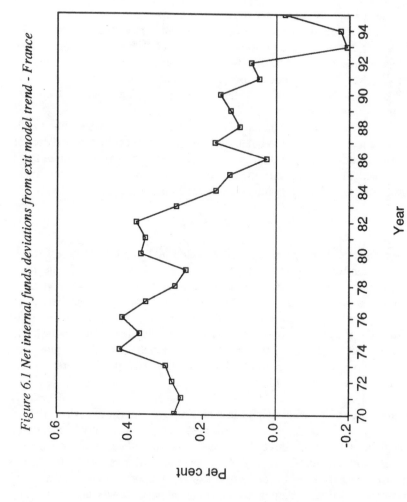

Figure 6.1 Net internal funds deviations from exit model trend - France

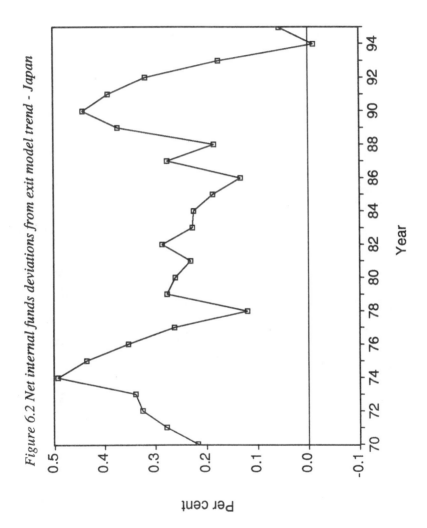

Figure 6.2 Net internal funds deviations from exit model trend - Japan

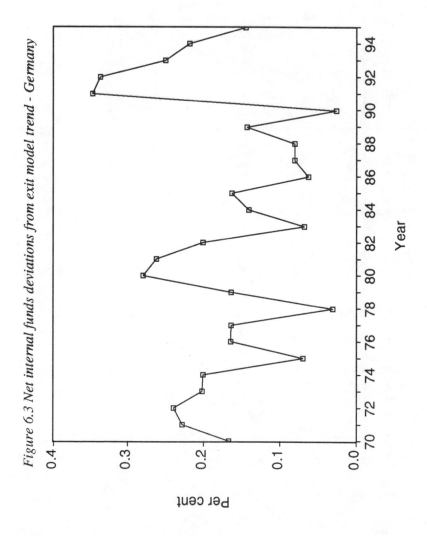

Figure 6.3 Net internal funds deviations from exit model trend - Germany

Table 6.2: Internal funds deviations – trend regressions: 1970–1995

Country	Gross Bank Finance as a Share of Gross Sources			Net Bank Finance as a Share of Net Sources		
	C	b_1	R^2	C	b_1	R^2
France	0.201	−0.005*	0.105	0.426	−0.018**	0.643
	(0.037)	(0.002)		(0.039)	(0.002)	
Japan	0.304	−0.013**	0.468	0.164	−0.006*	0.104
	(0.040)	(0.002)		(0.034)	(0.002)	
Germany	−0.006	0.002	0.032	0.164	0.001	−0.041
	(0.026)	(0.002)		(0.034)	(0.002)	

Notes:
a. Dependent variable is either deviations from the exit model trend of internal funds as a share of gross or net sources of funds.
b. Standard errors are in parentheses.
c. * indicates statistical significance at the 5 per cent level.
d. ** indicates significance at the 1 per cent level.

In order to test for the presence of trends in the deviations of shares of bank finance, these deviations were regressed against a time trend variable. As with the regressions involving internal funds shares, a negative trend for these deviations is indicative of convergence toward the exit model. The regressions were of the form:

$$BFDEV_t^i = C + b_1 T \qquad (6.14)$$

where $BFDEV_t^i$ is the deviation of the share of bank finance in country i in year t from that of the exit model trend, C is an intercept term, and T is a time trend variable. The results of these regressions are reported in Table 6.3. The regression results provide evidence for the claim that the French and Japanese financial systems are converging toward the exit model while the German system is not. The gross and net shares of bank finance in both France and Japan have statistically significant negative trends. Gross bank finance in Germany has a statistically significant positive trend while net bank finance displays no statistically significant trend. The results of these trend regressions were confirmed for every series, except for bank finance as a share of net sources for Japan, by performing tests for stationarity. The regression shows a significant negative trend while the test for the presence of a unit root suggests that the series is stationary.[16] Examining Figure 6.5 provides insight into this·result. The regression for the presence of a linear

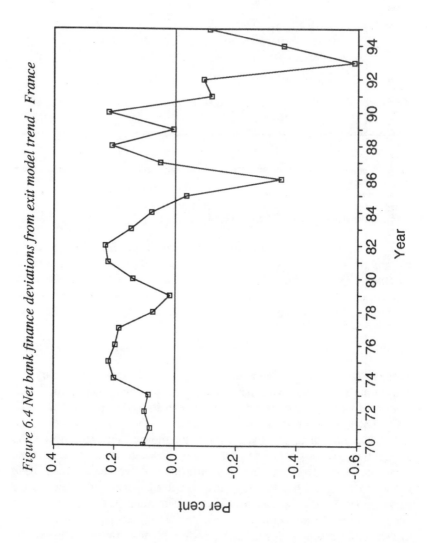

Figure 6.4 Net bank finance deviations from exit model trend - France

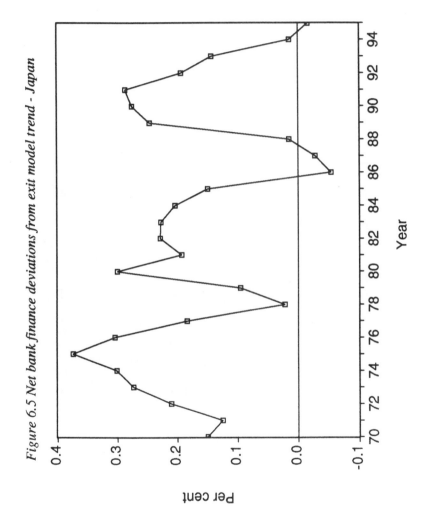

Figure 6.5 Net bank finance deviations from exit model trend - Japan

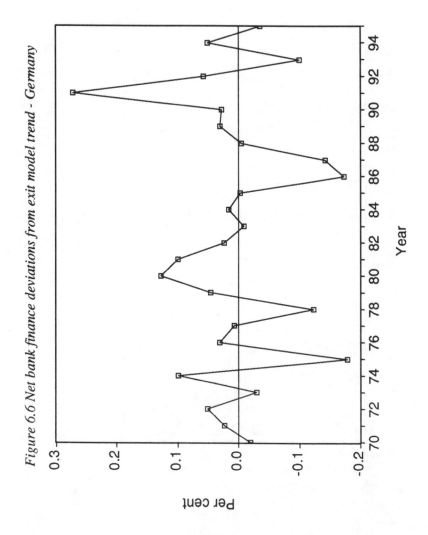

Figure 6.6 Net bank finance deviations from exit model trend - Germany

time trend is more sensitive to the endpoints than the test for stationarity and the recent decline is influencing the trend regression.

Table 6.3: Bank finance deviations – trend regressions: 1970–1995

Country	Gross Bank Finance as a Share of Gross Sources			Net Bank Finance as a Share of Net Sources		
	C	b_1	R^2	C	b_1	R^2
France	0.215	–0.009**	0.397	0.228	–0.015**	0.305
	(0.032)	(0.002)		(0.065)	(0.004)	
Japan	0.237	–0.004*	0.145	0.239	–0.005*	0.104
	(0.028)	(0.002)		(0.037)	(0.002	
Germany	0.068	0.004	0.121	–0.003	0.001	–0.042
	(0.028)	(0.002)		(0.037)	(0.003)	

Notes:
a. Dependent variable is either deviations from the exit model trend of gross or net bank finance as a share of gross or net sources of funds.
b Standard errors are in parentheses.
c. * indicates statistical significance at the 5 per cent level.
d. ** indicates significance at the 1 per cent level.

The examination of internal funds and bank finance as shares of gross and net sources of funds thus suggests that France and Japan have converged toward the exit model while Germany has not.

Uses of Funds

In order to assess further whether or not there has been any convergence in the patterns of uses of funds across financial systems, adjustments were made to the uses of funds. Trade Credit was subtracted from total uses of funds in order to make the data on uses of funds more comparable. This is referred to as adjusted uses of funds. As discussed earlier, the UK data on trade credit is not comparable to other countries' data on trade credit. It only covers part of import and export credit and leaves out all domestic trade credit. By measuring total uses of funds exclusive of trade credit, we bypass this problem and can focus our attention on the use of funds for physical investment and the purchase of financial assets.

Figure 6.7 plots the three-year moving average of investment as a share of adjusted uses for all five countries. Germany, Japan, and France have higher investment shares than the US and UK. Notably, France's investment share of adjusted uses falls over time, approaching the levels of the US and UK. Germany's investment share has remained high and stable while Japan's share has been high and has recently spiked upward. Figure 6.8 plots the standard deviation of investment as a share of adjusted uses in the five countries. The standard deviations are calculated and plotted for all of the countries as well as all of the countries excluding Japan. Both of these series are calculated by first taking a three-year moving average of each country's time series for the ratio of physical investment to adjusted uses of funds. Then, using this series for each country, a group standard deviation is calculated for each year in the same fashion as shown in equation 6.7. This is calculated both including and excluding Japan to show the impact of Japan's recent increase in its investment share. Both of these standard deviation series were formally tested for the presence of linear trends. These regressions took the form:

$$\sigma_{PI/AU} = C + b_1 T \qquad (6.15)$$

where $\sigma_{PI/AU}$ is the standard deviation series for either the ratio of physical investment to adjusted uses of funds for all five countries or exclusive of Japan, C is a constant term, and T is a time trend variable. A negative coefficient on the time trend variable indicates a negative trend for the standard deviation series and thus a convergence of the shares of investment in adjusted uses of funds for the group of countries in question. The results of these regressions are presented in Table 6.4.

When the group of five countries is considered, a positive trend is significant at the 5 per cent level of significance. This is particularly clear when examining the plot in Figure 6.8. The standard deviation is in general rising from 1976 to 1994. When Japan is excluded, a negative linear trend exists at the 5 per cent level of significance. Also, the standard deviation of the investment shares of the US, UK, France, and Germany have been falling steadily since 1988 as can be seen from Figure 6.8.[17] Japan's recent increase in its investment share is driving the standard deviation higher in the 1990s. There has been a recent convergence along the dimension of the share of adjusted uses of funds used for investment for Germany, France, the US, and the UK. Japan, however, has recently diverged from all of the other countries and has rapidly increased the share of adjusted funds used for investment.

Figure 6.9 plots the three-year moving average of the sum of stock and bond purchases as a share of adjusted uses. The UK and the US have much higher stock and bond purchases as shares of adjusted uses than Germany and Japan. France has shown a dramatic increase in its purchase of these financial assets. It begins with the lowest share of below 2 per cent

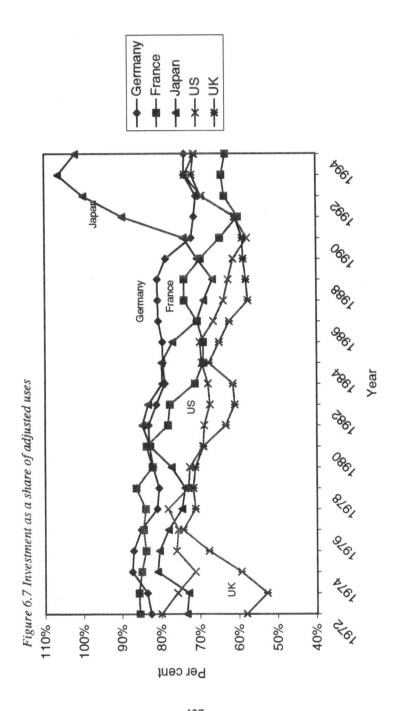

Figure 6.7 Investment as a share of adjusted uses

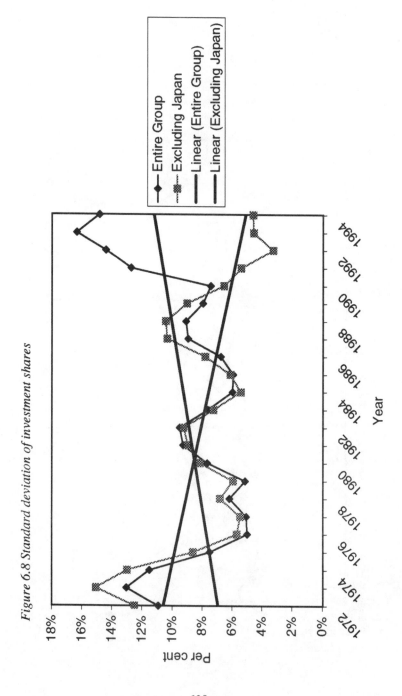

Figure 6.8 Standard deviation of investment shares

128

and ends the period with the highest share of 24 per cent. France has clearly converged to the levels of financial asset purchases found in the US and UK while Germany and Japan have not. To further illustrate this point the standard deviation of stock and bond purchases as a share of adjusted uses is plotted in Figure 6.10 for both the group of five countries and the group of only the US, UK, and France. These two plots diverge in the early 1980s with the standard deviation of the entire group rising nearly monotonically, while the standard deviation for the US, UK and France is falling considerably below that of the entire group. This is indicative of France's convergence toward the levels of financial asset purchases in the exit-dominated systems of the US and UK and the lack of such movement on the part of Germany and Japan. Both of these standard deviation series were formally tested for the presence of linear trends.

Table 6.4: Standard deviations of investment – adjusted uses of funds ratios: trend regressions 1972–1995

COUNTRIES	C	b_1	R^2
Entire Group	0.064	0.002*	0.129
	(0.013)	(0.0009)	
Excluding Japan	0.103	–0.002*	0.125
	(0.014)	(0.0009)	

Notes:
a. Dependent variable is either standard deviation of a three year moving average of the ratio of investment to adjusted uses of funds for the entire group of five countries or the group excluding Japan.
b. Standard errors are in parentheses.
c * indicates statistical significance at the 5 per cent level.
d. ** indicates statistical significance at the 1 per cent level.

These regressions took the form:

$$\sigma_{SB/AU} = C + b_1 T \qquad (6.16)$$

where $\sigma_{SB/AU}$ is the standard deviation series for either the ratio of stock and bond purchases to adjusted uses of funds for all five countries or exclusive of Japan and Germany, C is a constant term, and T is a time trend variable. A negative coefficient on the time trend variable indicates a negative trend for the standard deviation series and thus a convergence of the shares of investment in adjusted uses of funds for the group of countries in question. The results of these regressions are presented in Table 6.5

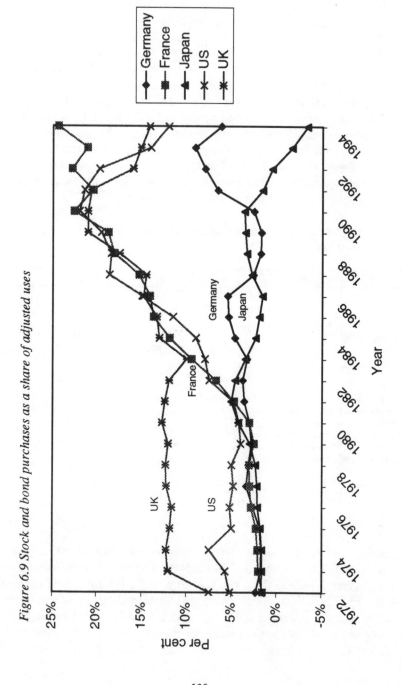

Figure 6.9 Stock and bond purchases as a share of adjusted uses

130

Figure 6.10 Standard deviation of stock and bond purchases as a share of adjusted uses

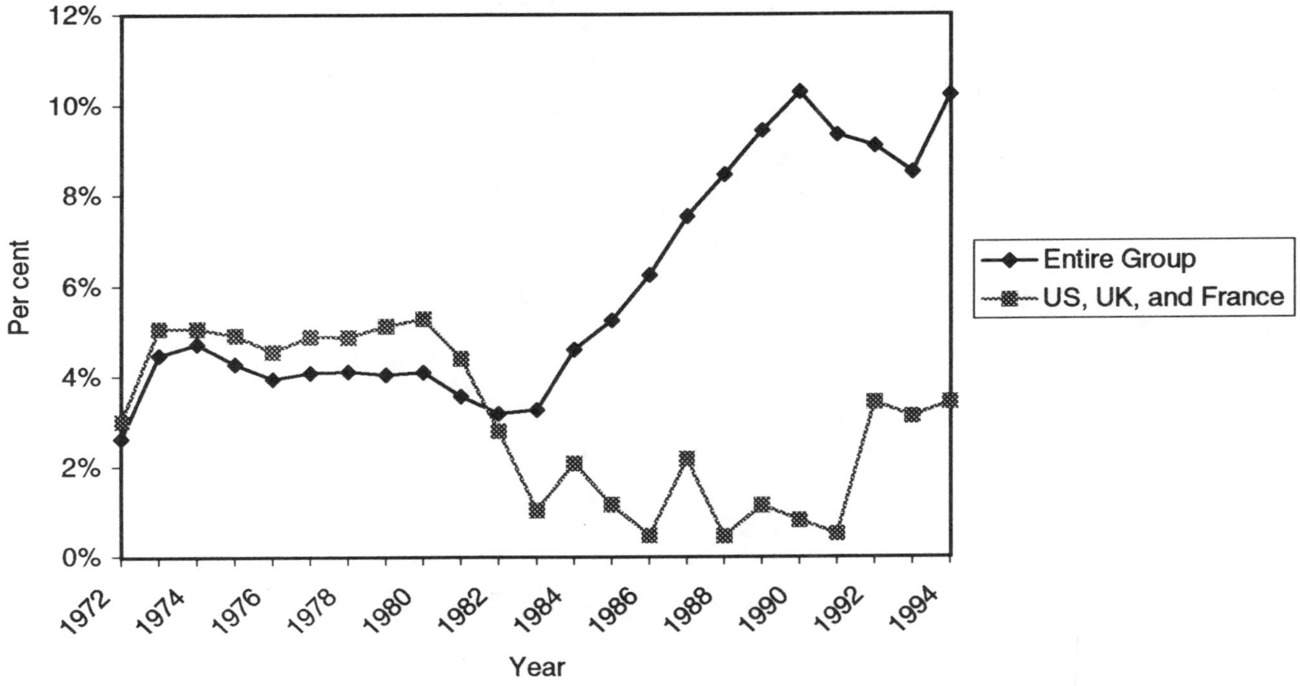

Table 6.5: Standard deviations of stock and bond purchases – adjusted uses of funds ratios: trend regressions 1972–1995[1]

COUNTRIES	C	b_1	R^2
Entire Group	0.015**	0.003**	0.716
	(0.005)	(0.0003)	
US, UK, & France	0.040**	–0.001**	0.366
	(0.005)	(0.0003)	

Notes:
a. Dependent variable is either standard deviation of a three-year moving average of the ratio of stock and bond purchases to adjusted uses of funds for the entire group of five countries or the group excluding Japan and Germany.
b. Standard errors are in parentheses.
c. * indicates statistical significance at the 5 per cent level.
d. ** indicates statistical significance at the 1 per cent level.

These time trend regressions indicate that at the 1 per cent level of significance there is a positive trend for the entire group and a negative trend for the US, UK, and France. These results are confirmed by stationarity tests.[18] This is evidence for the convergence of France and against the convergence of Germany and Japan along the dimension of the share of adjusted uses of funds going for the purchase of bonds and equities.

Overall, the uses data suggest that France has converged to the pattern of uses of funds found in the exit-dominated systems of the US and UK while Germany and Japan have not. Although Germany has shown a slow reduction in the share of funds used for investment, it still invests more than the US, UK, and France and it has continued to purchase fewer financial assets. Japan has recently diverged from the US and the UK by increasing its investment share and decreasing its purchase of financial assets.

CONCLUSION

What are the measurable differences in the patterns of financing sources and uses of funds across financial systems and is there any evidence of convergence of the voice-dominated financial systems toward the exit model? This chapter gave a new perspective to these questions. It provided recent evidence on the question of financial system convergence and shed light on differences in the patterns of uses of funds across financial systems that had not previously been examined.

Specifically, exit-dominated financial systems were found to invest less of their sources of funds than were voice-dominated systems. This chapter also showed that there has been strong evidence of convergence by France toward the US and UK along the uses of funds dimension. Germany and Japan showed no real evidence of convergence toward the exit model pattern of uses of funds.

In terms of convergence on the sources side, this chapter showed that France and Japan have been converging toward the exit model while Germany has not. France and Japan have decreased their reliance upon bank financing and have increased their use of internal funds as a source of financing. Germany's pattern of financing sources has remained quite stable and has shown no signs of convergence toward the exit model.

NOTES

1 The 1989 amendments extended the list of operations to be liberalized to include short-term capital movements as well as operations in forward, futures, options and swap markets.

2 In 1981 IBF's were created allowing Eurobanking on US soil free of reserve requirements, FDIC premiums, and state and local taxes. The initiation of IBF's caused an immediate shift of funds from offshore shell bank branches in places such as Nassau and the Cayman Islands back to the US (Sarver 1990). The Japanese counterpart to US IBF's, known as the Japanese offshore market though it is physically onshore, was established in 1985 (Coakley and Harris 1994).

3 A related measure, the Feldstein–Horioka condition, relies on the correlation of domestic quantities, savings and investment, though it presupposes all of the price measures; that is, it assumes all of the interest rate parity conditions hold (Frankel 1992). The literature on this condition begins with Feldstein and Horioka (1980) and includes Murphy (1984), Dooley, Frankel, and Mathieson (1987), Bayoumi (1990) and Blecker (1997).

4 Frankel (1990) discusses the removal of restrictions regarding capital flows in Germany in 1973-4, Japan in 1979-80, and the UK in 1979 and the subsequent disappearance of the differential between onshore and offshore rates of return on short-term assets. Blundell-Wignall and Browne (1991a and 1991b) provide time series of these differentials from the mid-1960s to 1990 for a wider group of countries. They show that these differentials disappeared in each of these countries, at different times, between the mid–1970s and the early 1980s.

5 Frankel (1990) found that, as of 1988, out of a group of twenty-three countries, only Greece, Bahrain, Malaysia, and South Africa deviated from covered interest parity to a significant degree. Short term rate differentials for major industrialized countries were nearly eliminated by 1991 (Frankel 1992). However, covered interest parity did not hold when capital controls were in place. See Frenkel and Levich (1975) and Frankel (1990).

6 See, among others, Froot and Frankel (1989), Fama (1984) and surveys by Levich (1985) and MacDonald and Taylor (1989)

7 McCallum (1994) argues that uncovered interest parity holds despite the failure of the unbiasedness hypothesis. Froot and Frankel (1989) and Frankel and Froot (1990) use survey data on expectations of exchange rate changes and find that uncovered interest parity holds.

8 See, among others, Cumby and Mishkin (1986) and Modjtahedi (1987).

9 Kasman and Pigott (1988) point out that the source of these differentials has changed with globalization: in earlier periods they were due to capital controls and when these controls were removed and exchange rates became flexible, the differentials became associated with expected exchange rate changes (Kasman and Pigott 1988, p. 42).

10 Zevin (1992) examines simple correlations of different variables for different time periods in the US, UK, Japan, and Germany. For his historical argument Zevin relies heavily on the work of Neal (1990) who studies the financial markets of seventeenth and eighteenth century Western Europe and finds that they were quite integrated. He writes 'today's movement from recently integrated international capital markets to an emerging global and cosmopolitan capital market seems to be recreating three centuries later, the conditions for the free transfer of private assets that existed for most of the eighteenth century in Western Europe'(Neal 1990, p. 231).

11 They note that 'in the past fifteen years banking and other financial service markets have undergone fundamental changes. In many cases national markets have moved from relatively stable environments, in which various types of firms operated in segmented markets protected by high regulatory barriers, to more fluid environments, in which market barriers are less restrictive and thus promote greater competition. The changes were often implemented through moves away from a relationship-based system of financial intermediation to one in which explicit market-based transactions predominated' (p. 257). Frankel and Montgomery go on to claim that it 'is now widely accepted that national reform efforts will not coalesce around a single model.'(p. 258).

12 Corbett and Jenkinson (1996) and Bertero (1994) address the issue of convergence by measuring the changing patterns of financing over time. Their analyses end in 1989 and 1991, respectively and neither provides any empirical work other than measuring how patterns of net sources of finance change over time.

13 The ADF test statistics were -3.286 for the series on gross internal funds, −3.223 for net internal funds, −4.100 for gross bank finance, and −2.822 for net bank finance. The McKinnon critical values are −3.749 at the 1 per cent level, −2.996 at the 5 per cent level, and 2.624 at the 10 per cent level. The presence of a unit root is thus rejected for all four series at the 5 per cent level for all of the series except for net bank finance that is rejected at the 10 per cent level.

14 See Schaberg (1997) for figures showing gross data.

15 ADF Test Statistics

Country	Share of Gross Sources	Share of Net Sources
France	−2.526	0.432
Japan	−1.940	−0.817
Germany	−2.642*	−2.854*

Notes: * indicates rejection at the 10 per cent level.

16 ADF Test Statistics

Country	Share of Gross Sources	Share of Net Sources
France	−2.099	−0.978
Japan	−2.574	−3.148**
Germany	−2.532	−3.353**

Notes: ** Indicates rejection of unit root at the 5 per cent.

[17] When these series were tested for stationarity, the results of the trend regressions were confirmed for the entire group but not for the group excluding Japan. The ADF test statistic for the former series was −2.477 and a unit root cannot be rejected but for the latter series the ADF test statistic is −4.516 which allows a unit root to be rejected at the 1 per cent level of significance. This is inconsistent with the linear trend regression, which is more sensitive to the endpoints, and is picking up the post-1988 decline in the standard deviation discussed above.

18 The ADF test statistic for the series for the standard deviation for the entire group was −0.148 and for the US, UK, and France it was −1.483. Both of these test statistics indicate that the hypothesis of the presence of a unit root cannot be rejected as the McKinnon critical value is −2.645 at the 10 per cent level.

APPENDIX

Table A6.1: Time trend regressions–bank finance: 1970–1995

Country	Share of Gross Sources			Share of Net Sources		
	C	b_t	R^2	C	b_t	R^2
Germany	0.266	–0.001	–0.194	0.177	–0.004	0.068
	(0.027)	(0.002)		(0.037)	(0.003)	
France	0.423	–0.016**	0.570	0.409	–0.020**	0.446
	(0.039)	(0.002)		(0.065)	(0.004)	
Japan	0.434	–0.010**	0.482	0.417	–0.010**	0.271
	(0.028)	(0.002)		(0.046)	(0.003)	
US	0.157	–0.005*	0.127	0.190	–0.006	0.052
	(0.036)	(0.002)		(0.060)	0.004	
UK	0.238	–0.005	0.075	0.170	–0.004	–0.017
	(0.044)	(0.003)		(0.070)	(0.005)	

Notes: Dependent variable is either gross or net bank finance as a share of total gross sources or as a share of total net sources. Standard errors are in parentheses. * indicates statistical significance at the 5 per cent level and ** indicates statistical significance at the 1 per cent level.

Table A6.2: Time trend regressions–internal funds: 1970–1995

Country	Share of Gross Sources			Share of Net Sources		
	C	b_1	R^2	C	b_1	R^2
Germany	0.585	−0.001	0.004	0.713	0.002	0.018
	(0.025)	(0.001)		(0.034)	(0.002)	
France	0.367	0.008*	0.186	0.446	0.022**	0.691
	(0.045)	(0.003)		(0.042)	(0.002)	
Japan	0.259	0.017**	0.510	0.543	0.011**	0.248
	(0.047)	(0.003)		(0.042)	(0.002)	
US	0.490	0.007**	0.236	0.760	0.010**	0.572
	(0.034)	(0.002)		(0.030)	(0.002)	
UK	).666	−0.003	0.020	0.996	−0.006	0.051
	(0.041)	(0.003)		(0.055)	(0.004)	

Notes: Dependent variable is either internal funds as a share of total gross sources or as a share of total net sources. Standard errors are in parentheses. * indicates statistical significance at the 5 per cent level and ** indicates statistical significance at the 1 per cent level.

7. Policies for the New Financial Environment

INTRODUCTION

Previous chapters demonstrated the convergence of financial systems along the dimensions of patterns of sources and uses of funds and the behaviour of and relationship between flows of financing and investment. These chapters have shown a convergence to a more speculative framework and a tendency toward lower and more volatile investment in the US, UK, and France and suggest the possibility of such developments in Germany and Japan if further convergence toward the exit model occurs. The first section of this chapter highlights these findings.

After summarizing these results, the second section explores some of their policy implications. One of the policy implications of the changes brought about by globalization is the further convergence of voice-dominated systems toward the exit-dominated model in the area of credit allocation and monetary policy. Globalization has brought about changes in the financial structures of these countries that have made their central banks use increasingly similar instruments of monetary policy in more liberalized and speculative financial environments.

In the past, monetary authorities often conducted monetary policy by directly controlling either the price or the quantity of credit or both. This was done with what are known as direct instruments of monetary policy. These direct instruments include interest rate controls, credit ceilings, and guided lending. Interest rate controls involve the government in directly regulating interest rates. For instance, deposit rates paid by banks may be capped at a certain level. Credit ceilings are established when the monetary authority places a direct limit on the amount of credit available. A credit ceiling is a quantity control on lending that often involves a target level of credit for the economy as a whole and the distribution of this total amount of credit to banks. Thus, each bank would have a specific quantity of credit it is permitted to supply. Penalties may be levied against banks that exceed their lending limit. Guided or directed lending programmes can involve the government directly lending to firms, usually at subsidized rates, or the provision of central bank credit at a discount to banks who make loans to preferred sectors. Direct credit allocation mechanisms have been nearly fully dismantled in countries with voice-dominated financial systems, such as France and Japan, where they used to be quite pervasive. Monetary authorities have adapted to changing financial structures and globalization by dismantling these and other types of direct controls and instead relying on similar indirect monetary policy instruments. Indirect instruments of monetary policy are designed to indirectly affect the price of credit. Three major classes of indirect instruments are open market operations, central bank lending, and reserve requirements.

These changes have left monetary authorities with more blunt instruments with which to engage in policy. Consequently, monetary policy, narrowly construed, may be ineffective in the new financial environment at allocating credit to productive uses. In this chapter, the effectiveness of monetary policy is explored in several ways. These include: the ability of countries to control interest rates and the impact of these subsequent interest rate changes on investment and economic activity, the changing nature of monetary policy channels, and the prospect of further convergence brought about by the completion of the European Monetary Union.

After summarizing the book's empirical evidence regarding the changing financial structures of the five countries and exploring the policy implications of these changes, the third section of the chapter then explores alternative policies to deal with the trends toward disintermediation, lower investment, and the increase in financial asset purchases. This chapter argues that the opportunity exists for the use of indirect monetary instruments in this era of globalization to achieve some of the allocative goals that were previously addressed by employing direct instruments. This chapter suggests examples of policies that could be part of an integrated package used to work through financial markets to help dampen speculation and promote productive investment. Some indirect instruments, such as reserve requirements on deposits, may be better suited than others to influence the domestic quantity of credit in a globalized environment. An argument here will be that setting reserve requirements on the asset side of financial firms' balance sheets at differential levels for different types of assets, as Pollin (1993) has most recently proposed for the US, provides an appropriately designed policy tool for credit allocation in increasingly globalized financial markets. As earlier chapters showed, exit systems have lower levels of productive investment. These chapters also showed that France has shown a steady convergence toward the exit model in its declining level of investment. This policy may help promote productive investment by providing a disincentive for financial institutions to lend for the purchase of stocks and other speculative activity.

This chapter also recommends regulatory changes, along the lines of those suggested for the US by D'Arista and Schlesinger (1993), that would bring the new forms of intermediation that have developed outside of the control of monetary authorities under their control. This policy approach complements the argument for new forms of credit allocation with indirect instruments. As discussed in the earlier chapters, bank lending has fallen as a source of funds for the non-financial business sector in France, the UK, and US. Subjecting non-bank intermediaries to the same regulations as banks, including the asset reserve requirements discussed above, would remove the regulatory advantage that these intermediaries have enjoyed and would allow monetary authorities to have influence over credit flows that have been outside of their purview. This influence could be used to help promote productive investment and discourage speculation. In addition to discouraging credit flows used for the purchase of financial assets, financial transactions could be discouraged as well. Taxing financial transactions, as proposed by Baker, Pollin, and Schaberg (1995), could help curb speculation and ease the problem of short-termism.

Some background is required before detailing these policy proposals. Therefore, the first section summarizes the dissertation's empirical evidence on the structural and behavioural differences across financial system types and the convergence of financial systems. It highlights evidence on the trends toward disintermediation, decreased investment, and the increasing purchase of financial assets. The second section explores the implications of this evidence for monetary policy and credit allocation policy. The third section details the three specific policy proposals designed to promote investment and reduce financial speculation. The final section concludes the chapter.

Summary of Empirical Results

This book's empirical work comparing the relationships between and the behaviour of flows of financing and investment across financial systems shows that clear differences exist between exit-dominated and voice-dominated financial systems. Evidence was presented showing that investment was more closely related to flows of funds in voice systems. These sources of funds were also demonstrated to be less volatile in voice systems, with bank finance playing a smoothing role in the aggregate sources of funds in these systems. The third chapter argued that these characteristics helped explain the fact that investment was both higher and less volatile in these voice systems.

The results of the empirical work in this book also indicate convergence of the voice-dominated systems of France and Japan toward the exit model and evidence that the US and UK are becoming even more extreme examples of countries with exit-dominated financial systems. First, there is a trend toward increased purchases of financial assets by the non-financial enterprise sectors of France, Japan, the US, and the UK. Second, there is a clear decrease in investment by the non-financial enterprise sectors of France, the US, and the UK and some evidence of such a pattern in Japan. Third, bank loans have fallen as a source of funds in both France and Japan while there have been periods of recent increases in bank loans to the non-financial enterprise sectors of the US and UK. A brief summary of the book's results on sources and uses of funds by the non-financial enterprise sectors in the five countries follows.

In the mid-1980s French firms began borrowing more in relation to their productive financing needs and using these funds to purchase financial assets. Investment for that sector fell from 70.2 per cent to 59.5 per cent of uses of funds from the period 1975-79 to the 1985-89 period. As investment was falling, purchases of equity shares increased from 1.9 per cent to 13.7 per cent of total uses.[1] Unlike in the US and UK, France's bank finance fell as a source of financing from 31.3 per cent of gross sources in 1975-79 to 16.9 per cent over the 1985-89 period.

Investment by the non-financial enterprise sector in Japan fell from 70 per cent of uses of funds in 1980-84 to 60.1 per cent in the period from 1985 to 1989. Over this same period, the purchases of stocks, bonds, and other financial assets increased from 1.0 per cent to 10.1 per cent of total uses of funds.[2] In Japan, firms and households borrowed more and purchased more financial assets creating a speculative bubble while fixed investment fell in the latter half of the 1980s (OECD 1989, p.101).

The German financial system does not display any similar patterns of convergence. Investment has remained quite stable as a use of funds and there has not been a significant increase in the purchase of equities by the non-financial business sector or a decrease in bank lending to this sector.

In the US, investment by this sector fell from 59.6 per cent of total uses of funds during the period from 1975-79 to 48.2 per cent in the period from 1985-89. At the same time, equity purchases rose from 4.4 per cent to 18.7 per cent of total uses and bank finance increased from 8.3 per cent to 10.6 per cent of gross sources.[3] US firms were borrowing more but investing less in physical assets while buying more stocks.[4]

The same pattern is found in the data on the sources and uses of funds for the non-financial business sector in the UK. Investment fell from 66.7 per cent of uses in the period from 1975-1979 to 56.7 per cent in 1985-1989. Over this same period, bank finance increased from 13.4 per cent to 27.6 per cent of gross sources of funds, and the purchase of equity increased from 8.0 per cent to 18.2 per cent of uses of funds. As in the US, firms in the UK were borrowing more but investing less while dramatically increasing their purchase of stocks.

POLICY IMPLICATIONS OF RESULTS ON GLOBALIZATION AND CONVERGENCE

The previous chapters discussed the significance of demonstrated differences in the patterns of sources and uses of funds, and the relationship between and behaviour of flows of financing and investment. Another reason differences in financial systems are significant is because the structure of voice-dominated systems allows for a greater degree of central bank control over the supply and allocation of credit as well as a long-term view regarding investment (Pollin 1995). One of the implications of the changes in financial structure documented in this book has been that some of the institutional structures that allowed for central bank involvement began to be dismantled. Thus, another aspect of convergence has been the movement away from government involvement in direct control over the supply of credit and its allocation in the voice-dominated systems.

This section explores the dismantling of direct credit allocation policies in voice-dominated financial systems. It also explores how the changes that have taken place in financial systems detailed in this book have affected the structure and effectiveness of monetary policy. One indicator of the effectiveness of monetary policy is the ability of monetary authorities to control certain interest rates.

Control of Interest Rates

It is difficult to see how financial market globalization would greatly affect the ability of monetary authorities to control key short-term interest rates. As long as banks are forced to hold central bank money, the market for these reserves will be insulated from the effects of globalization.[5] All of the central banks of the five countries studied here, with the recent exception of the UK, have reserve requirements and intervene in the market for reserves to influence their key short-term rates (Kasman 1992).

Therefore, the ability to control these short-term rates remains unaffected by globalization pressures. However, the desire of the central banks to adjust these rates and the consequences of these adjustments could be impacted on by financial market globalization.[6]

Globalization may not have reduced the ability of monetary authorities to control their key short-term rates, but has it weakened the link between these rates and other short-term market interest rates? Radecki and Reinhart (1988) investigate how globalization has affected the link between the federal funds rate and the three-month Treasury bill rate. In considering the determinants of the spread between these two rates, they found that foreign short-term rates were significant in explaining the spread. However, they did not find the influence of foreign rates to increase over time. They also found that a given change in borrowed reserves may have a larger impact on money market rates than in the past (Radecki and Reinhart 1988, p.26). In fact, most recent studies find that monetary policy affects short-term interest rates (Leeper and Gordon 1992; Christiano and Eichenbaum 1991).

If monetary authorities still have control over the interest rates on reserve funds and these rates have considerable influence on short-term market rates, then there is still the question of how these short-term rates impact on longer-term interest rates. While there is debate as to the strength of the effect, all studies reviewed here show some influence of short-term rates on long-term rates.[7] As Akhtar (1995, p. 121) points out, there is a dearth of recent studies that address the issue of possible shifts in monetary policy effects on long rates in recent years and few use data after 1983.[8] Blundell-Wignall et al (1985) found a decreasing long-run elasticity of long-term rates to short-term rates from the 1970s to the mid 1980s for the US, Japan, Germany, Italy, Canada, and the UK. Zevin (1992) finds that nominal government bond yields have shown the highest degree of correlation among many other interest rates and asset prices since 1960 while the yield curve is almost completely uncorrelated. This, along with the empirical literature on the relationship between short-term rates and long-term rates, is consistent with the view that central banks can't control long-term interest rates but can significantly impact on short-term rates. The evidence as to whether globalization has strengthened or weakened the impact of short-term rates on long-term rates is mixed, but suggests that the relative influence over the movement of long-term rates has shifted toward the growing global bond markets and away from monetary authorities.[9]

Changes in financial structure and the removal of quantity controls and interest regulations have led most monetary authorities to rely on market intervention to influence interest rates as their operating monetary policy strategy. Globalization of financial markets reduces the domestic constraints on funding availability for those borrowers able to tap larger global credit markets. This further reduces the role of quantity constraints and strengthens the role of interest rates as a rationing mechanism. Under a regime of floating exchange rates and free capital flows, monetary policy also operates through changes in the exchange rate. With evidence supporting the ability of monetary authorities to influence interest rates, the polar case of a small open economy in the Mundell–Flemming model does not seem appropriate for the major industrial economies.

A middle case in which monetary policy affects both interest rates and exchange rates is consistent with much of the empirical evidence that finds that monetary policy can affect interest rates and that it, in turn, affects exchange rates.[10] With flexible exchange rates and a high degree of capital mobility, the control of short-term rates bears the cost of exchange rate fluctuations. An expansionary monetary policy in the form of lower short-term rates will lead to capital outflow and currency depreciation. This depreciation can raise net exports. It is through this exchange rate channel that monetary policy is now supposed to function.[11] However, the speculative nature of foreign exchange markets yields the possibility for potentially costly swings in the value of the currency touched off by the expansionary policy. There is also the potential for the currency depreciation to touch off domestic inflation thus limiting the anticipated expansion of exports.[12]

The evidence from aggregate studies of the effect of interest rate changes on output is mixed. There is some evidence that the impact of interest rate changes on output has declined (Kahn 1989; Hirtle and Kelleher 1990). Other studies that include other channels of monetary policy in their examinations, however, have found no decline in the real economy's sensitivity to monetary policy (Mauskopf 1990; Mosser 1992).

Changes in financial systems and the removal of many quantity controls and interest ceilings have made central banks rely more heavily on indirect instruments to affect market interest rates and exchange rates to transmit monetary policy. There is, however, another channel, the lending channel, that could maintain its effectiveness in light of globalization. As will be seen, though, the lending channel is also weakened by globalization.

The Lending Channel

The basic argument for the existence of a lending or credit channel for monetary policy is that monetary policy has supply side effects on loan supply in addition to demand side effects caused by interest rate changes and the subsequent impact on components of demand. One of these components is credit demand.[13]   That is, monetary policy has an independent effect on the asset side of bank balance sheets.[14] If not all borrowers may substitute away from bank credit, then when tight monetary policy reduces the size of the banking sector's balance sheet it decreases the supply of credit available to those borrowers who are dependent upon banks for their credit needs. These are borrowers who are unable to seek financing from the domestic markets for bonds or commercial paper, the foreign markets or the Euromarkets.

This effect is likely weaker due to the globalization of financial markets because some borrowers can substitute away from domestic bank loans to other sources of funds. But clearly not all borrowers can do this. That is, the credit market is segmented and not all borrowers face the same opportunities for credit. Loans and bonds or loans and other sources of credit may be substitutes for some firms, but they are not in general perfect substitutes. It is the larger multinational firms that are more likely able to have a broader range of credit substitutes leaving smaller firms and borrowers trapped in their respective domestic credit structures. There is quite a bit of evidence to support the claim that small firms face significantly stronger liquidity constraints after a tightening of monetary policy.[15]   Globalization may be allowing larger firms to evade credit availability constraints during a monetary tightening if they are willing to pay a higher price, but many small and medium-sized firms are still subject to quantity constraints in credit markets. Thus the lending channel now operates more through changes in loan supply to smaller firms and on a smaller share of firms seeking credit.

This lending channel has also been weakened by changes in financial systems and globalization pressures that have led to a smaller share of funds being subject to reserve requirements and other types of control by monetary authorities.   This weakens the lending channel because policy changes, through either open market operations or changes in reserve requirements, now impact a smaller share of intermediated funds. Evidence that the lending channel has been weakened can be found by examining the sources and uses of funds for the non-financial business sector of the five countries studied here. In Chapter 2, bank loans were shown to be a small and shrinking source of funds for the exit-dominated systems of the US and UK. Japan and France showed a convergence toward the exit model along this dimension. Bank loans as a source of funds fell in Japan from 37.1 per cent of gross sources over the period from 1970-1974 to 24.3 per cent in 1990-1994. In France, bank finance fell from 35.4 per cent of gross sources to 8.3 per cent over the same period.[16] In both France and Japan firms have begun to rely less upon bank loans and more upon retained earnings as sources of funds. With bank loans comprising a shrinking source of funds for non-financial firms, the loan supply effect of monetary policy is weakened.

As the lending channel has been weakened by globalization, the effectiveness of monetary policy has also been influenced by globalization through its impact on the financial structures in which monetary policy is conducted. It is this change in the operating environments for monetary policy that are explored next.

Convergence of Monetary Policy Strategies and Operating Environments

Another dimension along which convergence has occurred is that of the institutional settings and operating strategies of monetary authorities. That is, largely as a result of financial market globalization, the instruments and channels of monetary policy in most industrial economies have converged. In a review of monetary operating procedures in the US, Japan, Germany, the UK, Canada, and Switzerland, Kasman (1992) found that their central bank intervention strategies were quite similar. Nearly all of them use interest rate operating targets.[17] He attributes this convergence to financial liberalization and innovation (p. 5). Icard (1994) discusses this notion of convergence: 'The globalization of markets is gradually making the way the various national financial systems operate, form expectations, and react the same. This inevitably leads to harmonization of national monetary policy characteristics, due to the growing uniformity of instruments and international coordination' (p. 93).

One of the aspects of the convergence of national financial systems is the increasingly similar ways in which monetary authorities conduct monetary policy. A common occurrence among these countries is the dismantling of direct monetary policy instruments and the movement to an almost singular reliance upon indirect instruments of monetary policy. The institutionally specific systems of direct policy instruments allowed central banks to play a role in directly influencing the quantity and allocation of credit. Changes in the financial structure of these countries conditioned changes in central bank operating strategies. These changes have also diminished the ability of authorities to control the quantity and influence the allocation of credit.

In the discussion in the previous chapters of other dimensions along which the financial systems of the major industrial countries have converged, it is also evident that globalization of financial markets has induced convergence with respect to the instruments and channels of monetary policy in these countries. Previously nationally distinct structures of quantity controls and administered prices have been dismantled and replaced with market-oriented methods for conducting monetary policy.[18] Central banks have witnessed the declining importance of intermediated credit, a growing turnover in financial markets, and the breakdown of the relationship between money and income and now use market interest rates both as operating targets and primary vehicles for the transmission of policy. Market operations have replaced quantity controls on lending as the main instrument of policy implementation. Globalization has affected the financial structures of these countries and the ways in which they conduct monetary policy. This is seen in the removal of the direct instruments that gave central banks considerable control over the supply and allocation of what was the major source of finance, domestic credit.

DISMANTLING DIRECT CONTROLS AND CREDIT ALLOCATION MECHANISMS

There has been a movement away from the involvement of the French and Japanese governments in credit allocation and direct measures of control over the credit supply. This retreat can be seen in the decreased reliance upon bank finance by French and Japanese firms discussed earlier in this chapter and at greater length in Chapter 2. Various government credit programes publicly subsidized some of that bank finance. As the French and Japanese governments dismantled their directed credit programes, it is not surprising that bank finance fell as a source of funds. This is evidence of an important dimension of the convergence of voice-dominated financial systems toward the exit model.

In Japan, the system of direct controls that existed in the 1970s as part of a strategy to influence the supply of bank credit has been mostly dismantled and monetary policy is now transmitted by indirect instruments focused on interest rate changes (Kasman and Rodrigues 1991). In the earlier period, when bank credit was the dominant source of financing, administrative controls on interest rate movements were in place and central bank credit was a major source of bank reserves. Central bank credit was supplied to banks that presented specific demands for credit for particular projects of their industrial customers in a process called 'window guidance'. This put the central bank in the position of monitoring not only the quantity of credit created but also its allocation. As the financial structure of Japan changed and became more globalized, banks were allowed to expand their funding sources both at home and abroad while domestic credit was becoming a much less important source of funds. As shown in Chapter 2, bank finance as a share of gross sources of funds for non-financial enterprises fell nearly 40 per cent in Japan from the 1970-1974 period to the period from 1990-1994.[19] Banks were able to expand their sources of funds domestically when they were allowed to issue certificates of deposit starting in 1979 and money market certificates beginning in 1985 (Calder 1997). Their ability to expand these sources by seeking funds overseas was encouraged by the relaxation of the laws governing foreign exchange transactions. The Foreign Exchange and Foreign Trade Control Law of 1948 and the Foreign Investment Law of 1950 prohibited all foreign exchange transactions unless expressly permitted by the government. These exchange control laws were beginning to be eroded in the 1970s. This erosion accelerated with the Foreign Exchange and Trade Control Law of 1980. It continued with the abolition in 1984 of the 'real demand' rule. This rule required banks to verify that all foreign exchange trades were based on real commercial transactions. The 1985 decision by Japan's Ministry of Finance to allow banks to directly engage each other in yen–dollar trades instead of through the eight regulated Tokyo foreign exchange brokers (Calder 1997) further eroded the exchange control laws. These changes in foreign exchange laws allowed Japanese banks and firms to gain access to funds overseas, particularly the Euromarkets, by the mid-1980s.

By the mid-1980s in Japan, banks no longer had to rely on credit from the central bank and firms no longer had to rely on credit from domestic banks. These factors combined to give the Bank of Japan less direct control over economic activity--it lost its leverage in using window guidance to affect the supply and composition of bank credit. As reliance on central bank credit declined, so did the use of discount window lending as a source of reserves. The practice of window guidance ended in 1982, and the end of the active use of reserve requirements as a policy tool followed soon after (Kasman and Rodrigues 1991). The Bank of Japan moved away from direct instruments that gave it considerable control over the quantity and allocation of credit. It has, instead, increasingly used indirect instruments of monetary policy aimed not at the domestic supply and allocation of credit but at interest rates. The indirect instruments of choice have been open market operations. The earlier heavy use of discount window lending and reserve requirements has been abandoned.

Similar changes have taken place in France. In earlier periods, the government was more heavily involved in directly controlling the supply and allocation of credit. Three–quarters of all loans to business in France in 1979 came from the state or semipublic financial institutions and their subsidiaries (Loriaux 1997). A system of credit ceilings imposed on private banks called *encadrement du crédit* allowed the government to play an allocative role by granting exceptions to these credit ceilings for preferred loans. This credit ceiling system was a principal tool of French monetary policy and allowed for specific increases in credit and allowed the money supply to be targeted for favoured uses. This system of credit ceilings was dismantled in France in early 1987 thus ending this particular credit allocation mechanism (Raymond 1992, p. 98). The principal focus of monetary control was no longer the quantity of credit given by banks but interest rates on the newly reformed money market. The development of the money market accelerated with the establishment of negotiable bank certificates of deposit in 1984, the establishment of new public short-term instruments, and the expansion of the previously small inter-bank money market to all firms (Loriaux 1997).

The French government further influenced the allocation of credit through subsidizing loans. This practice was diminished during the 1980s as the volume of subsidized credit declined. An example of this decline is the Economic and Social Development Fund. The fund provided industrial credit for investment projects and was a major supplier of industrial credit in the 1950s. The fund provided financing for 9 per cent of industrial capital investment in 1981 and only 0.29 per cent by 1992 (Loriaux 1997). Interest rate ceilings were removed and the administrative control over them was relinquished, the previously dependent central bank became independent, and the system of bank specialization was abolished allowing all French banks to have the same opportunities with respect to their activities (Bertero 1994). Interest rates have now become the main transmission mechanism for monetary policy in the French economy (Icard 1994, p.93; Raymond 1992, p. 99).

Convergence Toward a Single European Monetary Policy: The EMU

If and when the European Monetary Union is completed and the European Central Bank can set monetary policy for Europe, it will mark the complete convergence of the monetary policies of Germany, France, and the UK. Direct monetary financing of government deficits will no longer be possible. The completion of the EMU will also, by law, rule out quantitative credit controls and the regulation of interest rates. According to the terms of the Maastricht Treaty, the third stage of the European Monetary Union could have begun as early as 1997 if a majority of the member countries satisfied the convergence criteria established in the treaty.[20]

These conditions were not met by a majority of European countries by January 1, 1999. Therefore, the third stage of the union commenced with only as many countries as met the convergence criteria. This first part of stage three locked participating countries' currencies at existing exchange rates and the European Currency Unit began to be used in parallel with national currencies at these rates. The second part of stage three will replace these national currencies with a single circulating currency, the euro. At this point, the European Central Bank (ECB), headquartered in Frankfurt Germany, will, together with the national central banks that form the European System of Central Banks (ESCB), begin to function as *the* central bank for the union. The ECB will be in charge of the single union monetary policy. It will be an independent central bank governed by a Governing Council consisting of the central bank Governors of each participating country. The primary objective of the ECB, as laid out in the Maastricht Treaty, is price stability. Individual countries will no longer have monetary policy as a tool. There will be no ability to adjust exchange rates.

The completion of the EMU should be viewed as an opportunity to implement policies designed to work through the financial system to encourage investment and discourage speculation. The EMU could provide a Europe-wide institutional framework for implementing and overseeing these policies. The fact that agreements as to how banks would be regulated and by whom have not yet been made (Kregel 1993) provides an opening for the types of policy alternatives suggested in this chapter. These policies are now examined in greater detail.

POLICIES FOR THE NEW FINANCIAL ENVIRONMENT

This book has shown that globalization has led to structural changes in countries' financial systems. Changes have taken place in the financial structures of not only the voice-dominated systems but also exit-dominated systems like the US and UK. The empirical work in this book has demonstrated these changes. Evidence was presented showing a fall in bank loans as a source of funds in France and Japan. A fall in investment and an increase in the purchase of financial assets were also shown empirically for France, Japan, the US, and the UK. The diminished importance of domestically intermediated credit, lower investment, greater purchases of financial assets, and the growing volume of financial transactions have rendered the old policy tools less effective at promoting investment and discouraging excessive speculation. These structural changes have helped to alter the way monetary authorities conduct policy due to the convergence, along some dimensions, of their respective national financial systems.

The changes in financial structure and monetary policy methods have left monetary authorities with control over a smaller portion of the financial sector and with much more blunt instruments with which to engage in policy. The direct instruments that, in the past, were used by some central banks to influence the supply and allocation of credit, for the most part, no longer exist. What is needed is a utilization of indirect instruments in more effective ways that allow monetary authorities more sharply to influence both the supply and allocation of credit in the new financial environment as well as curb the tendency toward excessive turnover and speculation in financial markets. In this last section of the book, three specific policy proposals are put forward to address the particular problems of investment and speculation that have been discussed in light of the evidence that the book has presented on globalization and convergence of financial systems. One policy is designed to strengthen the lending channel for monetary policy. It complements a second policy, a proposal for an indirect method of credit allocation. This policy is designed to help channel funds toward investment and away from financial asset purchases. In order for this indirect instrument to be used effectively, the common problem facing monetary authorities of growing disintermediation and diminished control over the financial system needs to be addressed. I have addressed this problem with a proposal to strengthen the lending channel. A third policy, a tax on financial transactions, is aimed directly at reducing speculation in financial assets.

Regain Control and Strengthen the Lending Channel

Globalization has led to a higher degree of disintermediation. Domestic bank lending is becoming a less important source of funds and this has left monetary authorities with control over a smaller portion of the flow of financing. This reduces the strength of the lending channel and renders problematic policies aimed at increasing the domestic supply of credit, such as lowering reserve requirements. With a smaller share of funds intermediated through the traditional banking sector and subject to reserve requirements, changes in these required reserve ratios will have a smaller effect on loan supply. This smaller loan supply effect also holds for open market operations. The declining share of funds against which reserves must be held leads to a decreased ability of monetary authorities to affect the supply of loans. The decline of domestically intermediated funds and the formation of what D'Arista and Schlesinger (1993), in discussing the

US case, call the 'parallel banking system' has affected many countries. It has reduced the leverage of monetary authorities as the pool of funds against which reserves must be held has shrunk as a share of total funds.

These parallel systems have put pressure on monetary authorities to lower reserve requirements because institutions that are required to hold reserves are put at a cost disadvantage in comparison with those which are not obligated to hold reserves. The growth of the Euromarkets has provided a significant source of this pressure. What is needed, across countries, is a system, like that proposed for the US by D'Arista and Schlesinger (1993), that subjects all institutions that either make or sell loans or engage in the acceptance of funds from the public to the same requirements as to the holding of reserves with the central bank. The French Bank Law of 1984 has already defined all French financial institutions that engage in deposit-taking or the making or selling of loans as credit institutions and placed them under the same regulations (Bertero, 1994). A broad agreement among countries to this policy, as was achieved with respect to capital adequacy requirements in the Basel accords, and an agreement about the appropriate range for reserve requirements, would be beneficial in two ways. First, it would allow monetary authorities to regain control over the flow of funds. Second, it would put an end to the regulatory arbitrage that pits one country's regulations, in this case the level of required reserves, against another's in the attempt to attract or maintain financial firms. The European Commission has already acknowledged the problem of regulatory arbitrage and has sought to reduce it by agreements related to the EMU. The Commission's directives concerning competition in banking and financial services state that the prudential regulations applied in individual countries will apply to all institutions operating in those countries (Kregel, 1993). This is designed to prevent regulatory competition among European countries. With all of these policies in place, monetary authorities would be able to use reserve requirements in a more active fashion to influence the supply of credit. The lending channel would be strengthened as both open market operations and reserve requirement changes would have a larger impact on credit supply.

If one accepts the proposition that loans and bonds are imperfect substitutes for some classes of borrowers, then it is possible to construct policies aimed at increasing domestic credit availability for those firms that are unable to take advantage of the sources of funds made newly available by globalization. If the market for bonds and the market for bank loans are somewhat segmented, then it is possible to target the market for loans by adjusting reserve requirements on deposits.[21] The use of reserve requirements as a monetary policy tool in France illustrates this possibility. In France, changing the reserve requirement makes it possible to reduce the link between external and domestic effects of monetary policy (Icard 1994). Lowering reserve requirements allows the French authorities to offset interest rate increases aimed at stabilizing the franc.[22] Lowering reserve requirements increases the willingness of intermediaries to supply credit at any given interest rate. If credit is rationed, changes in the quantity of reserves in the banking system through, for example, open market operations lower the cost of funds for banks. Banks can respond by lending funds to those who were previously rationed without changing the interest rate. Thus, changes in credit supply are possible without large changes in interest rates. This creates a way for monetary authorities to influence domestic credit conditions without the fear of large bond sales or purchases triggered by interest rate changes that would work through interest rate and exchange rate channels and potentially result in unwanted currency and price fluctuations. The Bundesbank in Germany has also used reserve requirements in this way. In 1980, facing capital outflows to the US and UK and the beginning of a recession, the Bundesbank felt it could not lower interest rates for fear of greater capital outflows. Instead, it chose to lower reserve requirements to stimulate domestic liquidity.[23] Germany's use of reserve requirements as an active monetary policy tool is made easier and more effective because its definition of what constitutes a bank is broader than, for example, in the US and thus a greater share of funds is subject to the Bundesbank's reserve requirements. Reserve requirements could be lowered on their own, leaving interest rates unchanged, to increase the quantity of domestic lending. The use of reserve requirements to influence the supply of credit is also increasingly appealing because as banks act to match their assets and liabilities which bear market interest rates, their activity becomes less sensitive to changes in interest rates. The regained ability to use reserve requirements as an active tool will help strengthen the lending channel. This, coupled with the continued ability to affect short-term rates through open market operations and credit supply through the lending channel, will leave monetary authorities in a stronger position to influence the quantity of credit available domestically.

Allocate Credit Using Indirect Instruments

A stronger lending channel brought about by increased monetary authority control over forms of intermediation that have developed outside of their control will help give them more control over the quantity of credit. However, given changes in financial structures and the tendency toward financial churning and speculation, will increases in credit result in productive investment?   Voice-dominated financial systems had institutional structures in place to encourage the channelling of credit toward productive uses. Globalization has changed national financial structures and the ways in which monetary authorities conduct monetary policy, but monetary authorities still have the ability to influence domestic interest rates, particularly on the short end of the yield curve, independently of foreign rates. In this sense, the effectiveness of monetary policy has not been severely reduced by globalization of financial markets. However, declining control over long-term interest rates and growth in the use of credit to fund speculative purchases of already existing assets, as opposed to the productive funding of new assets, puts several points of the effectiveness of monetary policy into question.

The institutional structures and direct instruments that allowed central banks in countries like Japan and France to influence the allocation of credit in favour of productive investment have been largely dismantled. Differential asset reserve requirements like those proposed for the US most recently by Pollin (1993) can be used to regain the ability to influence the allocation of credit in the context of globalization and changing financial structures.   This policy, combined with the first proposal to 'level the playing field' for all financial firms, would markedly strengthen monetary authorities' ability to allocate credit.   This new structure for credit allocation is well suited for the more complex financial structures that have evolved. This is because it allocates credit via indirect instruments and, coupled with the strengthening of the lending channel, is able to influence the flow of credit through non-bank intermediaries.

The indirect method of credit allocation involves the application of reserve requirements to the asset side of all financial firms' balance sheets at different rates for different types of assets. These differences in asset reserve requirements could be altered to favour the funding of certain types of assets over others. Classes of preferred assets would need to be defined and a target ratio of preferred assets to total assets would need to be set. Then, in order for the system to be more flexible, the requirements should be implemented as first proposed by Maisel (1973). That is, as a system of permits that can be auctioned in a market rather than quotas. Institutions that have preferred assets in excess of the specified target could be issued a permit for that excess amount of preferred assets which they could then sell to financial firms whose preferred assets fall below the target.   A policymaking process, involving as much democratic participation as possible, would have to be developed that would determine what activities would be selected to qualify as preferred assets.

The effect of this policy would be that financial intermediaries that funded preferred productive investment, such as the purchase of new plant and equipment, would face lower reserve requirements on these assets than those financial firms that funded more non-preferred assets such as the purchase of stocks, other financial assets, or commercial real estate. This raises the cost to intermediaries of funding undesired activity relative to productive investment and provides an indirect instrument for credit allocation. In doing so, this policy model provides a simple and flexible system aimed at influencing the allocation of credit. This system would replace the dismantled systems of direct controls, like the *encadrement du crédit* in France or strict window guidance in Japan. The system could also replace some of the functions that used to be carried out by narrowly construed intermediaries charged with providing credit to specific types of borrowers or for specific projects. Some of these institutions have disappeared as financial liberalization measures have removed restrictions on the types of activities in which these intermediaries can engage. Instead of providing credit to preferred sources through compartmentalized institutions, differential asset reserve requirements can be used to give preferential treatment to certain types of assets regardless of the institution that holds the assets.

Tax Financial Transactions

The development of more active capital markets in voice-dominated financial systems and the growing volume of financial transactions present the possibility that the problem of short-term bias that exists in exit-dominated systems will begin to emerge in voice-dominated systems as they converge toward the exit model. At least as far back as Keynes, economists have worried that the possibility of achieving short-term gains through speculation on financial markets might obstruct their ability to carry through their more basic function. As a way to address this problem Keynes advocated a small tax on the transfer of securities to slow down the rate at which shares change hands. He hoped that this would encourage asset holders to pay more attention to the long-term prospects of the companies whose stocks and bonds they held, and less attention to transient factors and rumours which may govern price fluctuations at any point in time.

There has been a rapid increase in financial transactions relative to output in both exit-dominated systems like the US and UK and voice-dominated systems like Germany, Japan, and France that are experiencing greater turnover in their newly growing capital markets. For example, the value of the volume of financial transactions in stocks and bonds in France rose from 124 billion francs to 3,806 billion Francs in 1990. This increase in volume corresponds to an increase in turnover--value transacted divided by value outstanding--from 0.15 in 1980 to 0.878 in 1990. This implies a decrease in the average holding period of these assets from nearly seven years to just over one year.[24] This trend is likely to continue in the voice-dominated systems as their capital markets deepen. The growth in financial market churning in voice-dominated systems may begin to erode their longer-term view of investment projects and increase the problem of short-term bias typical of exit-dominated systems.

A small tax on financial transactions would both help lower the likelihood of this short-term bias developing in voice-dominated systems as well as reduce the short-termism in exit-dominated systems. One specific type of transactions tax is the 'Tobin Tax' (ul Haq et al. 1996). This is a small tax on foreign exchange transactions proposed by James Tobin. It is designed to reduce speculation and volatility in the foreign exchange market. The securities transactions tax proposed here is a more general securities tax applied to a broader range of securities transactions including equity, debt, and derivative transactions. The purpose of such a tax would be to raise the cost of trading financial assets and thereby reduce speculative activity. The tax should be small enough that it would be negligible when the asset purchased was held for a long period of time but rather more costly for those who trade frequently. For example, a securities transaction tax structure could tax equity trades at 0.5 per cent of the value of the transaction.[25] This tax represents a smaller share of the anticipated return the longer the investment horizon of the investor.

Many countries have had securities transaction taxes in place at various points in time but have been pressured to lower or remove these taxes as they face competition from other countries that do not have these taxes and are thus more attractive places for financial firms to conduct their business.[26] This phenomenon of regulatory competition, like that in the case of reserve requirements and central bank control, calls for an agreement among countries to the implementation of a uniform securities transaction tax. The more countries that agree to the implementation of securities transaction taxes, the less of a problem there will be with tax evasion through movement of operations abroad. While it may be possible for large countries with deep and established financial markets, like the US, to tax securities transactions without fear of losing many financial firms, smaller countries face a more serious exit constraint. All countries implementing the tax will see reductions in trading volume depending on the price elasticity of the various securities transactions being taxed. A well-designed securities transactions tax could both raise revenue and decrease turnover and speculation in financial markets.

Revenue from the tax could be used to fund public investment projects that would crowd in private investment. Taxing financial transactions coupled with using differential asset reserve requirements that create disincentives for providing credit for speculative uses can be coupled to help tilt the playing field toward productive investment and away from speculation.

CONCLUSION

Globalization has made conducting monetary policy and allocating credit more difficult. It has brought about changes in financial structures that were discussed at length throughout the book and highlighted here. These changes include the reduction of bank finance as a source of funds in France and Japan, the increased purchases of financial assets and reduction in investment in the US, UK, and France, increased turnover in financial markets, and disintermediation from traditional banks under the control of monetary authorities. These changes have induced responses by monetary authorities. They have led to the use of similar indirect instruments of monetary policy and the dismantling of institutional mechanisms for credit allocation. Monetary authorities have been left with less control over the flow of financing.

The argument of this chapter has been that regulatory changes and new policy instruments are needed to increase monetary policy effectiveness and help allocate credit to productive investment while dampening speculative pressures in the new financial environment. The new forms of intermediation that have developed need to be brought under the control of monetary authorities. With this regained control over the channeling of credit, monetary authorities should use differential asset reserve requirements, an indirect policy tool suited for the changed financial environment, to allocate credit toward productive investment. A tax on financial transactions working together with these differential asset reserve requirements could be used to help curb speculation and promote investment. These three policies should be seen as part of an integrated package that countries could use to intervene through financial markets to promote productive investment and reduce speculation.

NOTES

1 This evidence is consistent with that presented by the OECD which shows that the share of financial investment in total enterprise expenditures rose from 2.6 per cent in 1979 to 33.6 per cent in 1985 and higher in the later 1980s (OECD, 1987 p. 53).

2 Calculations made from *National Accounts Table for Account 1-Non-Financial Incorporated Enterprises* published by the Economic Planning Agency of Japan. See Chapter 2 for further details on uses of funds in Japan.

3 Data on sources and uses of funds for US are from *Federal Reserve Board Flow of Funds Accounts Table F. 102*. See Chapter 2 for more information on sources and uses of funds in the US.

4 In the US, with a vigorous market for corporate control, credit was used to purchase shares in takeovers (Crotty and Goldstein 1993; Pollin 1995). Crotty and Goldstein (1993) discuss that in the US by 1988 several large New York banks were channeling as much as 40 per cent of their new commercial loans into LBO's. The changing structure of corporate balance sheets in the US in the 1980s points to this use of funds as well. Over those ten years a net $622 billion in equity was removed from the corporate sector's balance sheet. Net credit market borrowing was $1289 billion while fixed investment exceeded the internally available funds to corporations by $99 billion (Crotty & Goldstein, pp. 255, 268). This suggests a considerable amount of borrowing undertaken by the corporate sector was used to purchase shares and other existing assets.

5 See Radecki and Reinhardt (1988), Goodfriend (1991), and Poole (1991).

6 As will be discussed later in this section, the central banks of Germany, France, and the UK would lose their ability to independently control short-term rates and monetary policy more generally if and when the European Monetary Union is completed.

7 Pollin (1991) shows evidence of an interactive effect whereby short-term rates impact long-term rates but long-term rates also influence short-term rates. For evidence on the impact of short rates on long rates see Blanchard (1984), Estrella and Hardouvelis (1990), Campbell and Shiller (1991), Cohen and Wenninger (1994), Cook and Hahn (1989), Hardouvelis (1994), Mankiw (1986) , Radecki and Reinhart (1994). For an excellent review of the empirical literature on the relationship between monetary policy and long-term interest rates see Akhtar (1995).

8 This is with the exception of Radecki and Reinhart (1994) and Cohen and Wenninger (1994) who use data up to 1993.

9 This is consistent with Pollin (1991) who suggests that long-term interest rate trends may create an environment for central bank determined short-term rates to follow.

10 In addition to the above evidence on interest rates, Eichenbaum and Evans (1993) employ VAR analysis and find that, during the flexible exchange rate era, expansionary shocks to US monetary policy led to sharp persistent depreciations in both nominal and real US exchange rates as well as significant and persistent increases in the spread between foreign and US interest rates. This is consistent with the view that monetary policy affects both interest rates and exchange rates.

11 In general, sectoral studies of the incidence of monetary policy in the US have found that it has shifted from the housing sector toward net exports. Bosworth (1989) argues that housing has become less interest elastic while net exports have become increasingly interest sensitive. Kahn (1989) also finds decreased interest sensitivity of housing and increased interest sensitivity of net exports. Housing was also found to be less interest elastic by Friedman (1989). In smaller countries, where net exports comprise a much larger share of output, the net export channel has been important for monetary policy for a longer period of time.

12 Dornbusch and Giovinnini (1990) argue that these effects have often been exaggerated. Goodman (1992), however, in looking at the experience in Western Europe since the advent of floating exchange rates, believes that these inflation effects have not been insignificant.

13 For a discussion of the lending channel see Tobin and Brainard (1963) and Bernanke and Blinder (1988).

14 In the framework of Greenwald and Stiglitz (1991), decreasing reserve requirements has the effect of increasing banks' willingness to lend at any given interest rate. This credit availability effect is a direct effect on loan supply that is not mediated through changes in interest rates on bonds (Stiglitz 1992b, p 300). Thus monetary policy is able to have real effects on output· without requiring large interest elasticities of demand (Blinder and Stiglitz 1983). Stiglitz argues that this view of monetary policy provides an explanation as to why monetary policy appears to be effective in small open economies and not just because of changes in exchange rates:

The fluctuations in output are supply, not demand driven. And our theory emphasizes that while markets for government T-bills may work quite well, capital for loan purposes does not flow so freely. Monetary policy can affect the credit institutions within a country, and by that means, have a real effect on the economy. (Of course, even that effect may get weakened, as multinational firms switch their borrowing from banks in one country to another). (Stiglitz 1992b, pp. 302-3)

Implicit in this view is the notion that bonds and loans are not perfect substitutes. This lending view of monetary policy does not mean that direct effects of interest rates on demand are unimportant or that open market operations and interest rate changes don't also impact on loan supply. Rather, it just means that they are not necessary for monetary policy to be effective

15 See Gertler and Hubbard (1988), Gertler and Gilchrist (1994) and Kashyap, Lamont and Stein (1994).

16 Economic Planning Agency of Japan and *OECD Financial Statistics Part 2*. See Chapter 2 for further details on sources of funds.

17 This move toward indirect instruments of monetary policy is not confined to the major OECD countries discussed here. For a discussion of this phenomenon in developing countires see Alexander, Balino and Enoch (1995).

18 For a review of the structure of Japan and France's earlier monetary control mechanism see Kasman and Rodrigues (1991) and Loriaux (1991) respectively.

19 Calculation based on sources of funds data from Economic Planning Agency of Japan. See Chapter 2 for details on sources of financing.

20 The convergence criteria are: 1) a deficit/GDP ratio of below 5 per cent and a debt/GDP ratio of below 60 per cent, 2) observance of the normal fluctuation margins provided for in the Exchange Rate Mechanism (ERM) for at least two years without actively devaluing currency, 3) long-term nominal interest rates within 2 per cent of the three best performing countries in terms of price stability, 4) inflation within 1.5 per cent of the three best performing countries.

21 It would also be possible to use differential asset reserve requirements to target credit to these borrowers. The point here is that adjusting reserve requirements on domestic deposits will have a somewhat targeted effect on those borrowers that are constrained to obtain bank loans from domestic institutions.

22 Icard (1994) writes 'in October 1991, for instance, the rise in the Banque de France's key rates, intended to stabilize the franc within the ERM band, was combined with a cut in reserve requirements that avoided the need to raise the minimum bank lending rate. A variety of similar, or reverse, steps have been taken successfully in recent years' (p. 101).

23 This policy choice is described in the 1981 Joint Economic Committee of the US Congress report 'Monetary Policy, Selective Credit Policy, and Industrial Policy in France, Britain, West Germany, and Sweden.'

24 Author's calculations based on figures from Bertero (1994).

25 Baker, Pollin, and Schaberg (1995) detail a structure for a securities transaction tax in the US. This structure begins with a 0.5 per cent tax rate for equity trades and recommends lower tax rates for debt and derivative transactions.

26 Baker, Pollin, and Schaberg (1995) describe the pressures to remove these taxes in various countries in order to attract financial firms.

References

Akhtar, M.A. (1995), 'Monetary Policy and Long-Term Interest Rates: A Survey of Empirical Literature', *Contemporary Economic Policy*, **13** (July), pp. 110-130.

Ahktar, M.A. and E.S Harris (1987), 'Monetary Policy Influence on the Economy--An Empirical Analysis', *Federal Reserve Bank of New York Quarterly Review*, (Winter), pp. 19-31.

Alexander, W.E., T. Balino and C. Enoch (1995), 'The Adoption of Indirect Instruments of Monetary Policy', *IMF Occasional Paper* No. 126.

Allen, Roy (1994), *Financial Crises and Recession in the Global Economy*, Aldershot, UK and Brookfield, US: Edward Elgar.

Applebaum, Eileen and Peter Berg (1995), 'Financial Market Constraints and Business Strategy in the US', manuscript, Economic Policy Institute.

Baker, Dean, Robert Pollin and Marc Schaberg (1995), 'The Case for a Securities Transaction Tax: Taxing the Big Casino', manuscript, Department of Economics, University of California-Riverside.

Bayoumi, T. (1990), 'Saving–Investment Correlations: Immobile Capital, Government Policy, or Endogenous Behaviour?' *International Monetary Fund Staff Papers*, **37**, pp. 360-87.

Bennett, P. (1990), 'The Influence of Financial Market Changes on Interest Rates and Monetary Policy: A Review of Recent Evidence', *Federal Reserve Bank of New York Quarterly Review*, (Summer), pp. 8-30.

Berglöf, Eric (1990), 'Capital Structure as a Mechanism of Control: A Comparison of Financial Systems,' in M. Aoki, B. Gustafsson and O.E. Williamson (eds), *The Firm as a Nexus of* Treaties, London: Sage Publications, pp. 237-62.

Bernanke, B. and A. Blinder (1988), 'Credit, Money, and Aggregate Demand', *American Economic Review*, **78** (May), pp. 435-9.

Bertero, E. (1994), 'The Banking System, Financial Markets, and Capital Structure: Some New Evidence from France', *Oxford Review of Economic Policy*, **10** (4), pp.68-78.

Blanchard, O.J. (1984), 'The Lucas Critique and the Volcker Deflation', *American Economic Review*, **74** (May), pp. 211-5.

Blecker, Robert (1997), 'Policy Implications of the International Saving–Investment Correlation', in R. Pollin (ed.), *The Macroeconomics of Finance, Saving and Investment*, Ann Arbor: University of Michigan Press.

Blinder, A. and J. Stiglitz (1983), 'Money, Credit Constraints, and Economic Activity', *American Economic Review*, **73** (May), pp. 297-302.

Blundell-Wignall, A. and F. Brown (1991a), 'Increasing Financial Market Integration, Real Exchange Rates and Macroeconomic Adjustments', *OECD Department of Economics and Statistics Working Paper* No. 96, (February).

Blundell-Wignall, A. and F. Brown (1991b), 'Macroeconomic Consequences of Financial Liberalisation: A Summary Report', *OECD Department of Economics and Statistics Working Paper* No. 98, (February).

Blundell-Wignall, A., F. Brown, and P. Manasse (1985), 'Monetary Policy in the Wake of Financial Liberalisation', *OECD Economics and Statistics Department Working Paper* No. 77, (April).

Bond, S., Elston, J. Mairsse and B. Mulkay (1995) 'A Comparison of Empirical Investment Equations Using Company Panel Data for France, Germany, Belgium, and the UK', Mimeo, Oxford University.

Borio, C. (1990), 'Patterns of Corporate Finance', *BIS Economic Papers* **27**, Basel: Bank for International Settlements.

Bosworth, B. (1989), 'Institutional Change and the Efficacy of Monetary Policy', *Brookings Papers on Economic Activity*, **1**, pp. 77-125.

Bulow, J. and J. Shoven, (1978), 'The Bankruptcy Decision,' *Bell Journal of Economics*, **9**, pp. 437-56.

Cable, J. (1985), 'Capital Market Information and Industrial Performance: The Role of West German Banks', *The Economic Journal*, **95** (March), pp. 118-32.

Calder, Kent (1997), 'Assault on the Bankers' Kingdom: Politics, Markets, and the Liberalization of Japanese Industrial Finance', in Loriaux et al. (eds), *Capital Ungoverned: Liberalizing Finance in Interventionist States*, Ithaca: Cornell University Press.

Calomaris, C.W., C.P. Himmelberg, and P. Wachtel, (1995), 'Commercial Paper and Corporate Finance: A Microeconomic Perspective', *Carnegie–Rochester Conference Series on Public Policy*, **42**, pp. 203-55.

Cameron, Rondo (1967), *Banking in the Early Stages of Industrialization*, New York: Oxford University Press.

Campbell, J. and R.J. Shiller (1991), 'Yield Spreads and Interest Rate Movements: A Bird's Eye View', *Review of Economic Studies*, pp. 495-514.

Capoglu, G. (1994), 'The Internationalization of Financial Markets and Competitiveness in the World Economy', *Journal of World Trade*, pp.111-118

Carpenter, Robert E., Steven M. Fazzari, and Bruce C. Petersen (1994), 'Inventory Investment, Internal–Finance Fluctuations, and the Business Cycle', Brookings Papers on Economic Activity, **2**, pp. 75-137.

Carrington, John C. and George T. Edwards (1979), *Financing Industrial Development*, New York: Praeger.

Cerny, P.G. (1994), 'The Dynamics of Financial Globalization: Technology, Market Structure, and Policy Response', *Policy Sciences*, **27**, pp. 319-342.

Cho, Y.D. (1995), 'Financial Factors and Corporate Investment: A Microeconometric Analysis of Manufacturing Firms in Korea', Dphil Thesis, University of Oxford.

Christiano, L. and M. Eichenbaum (1991), 'Identification and the Liquidity Effect of a Monetary Policy Shock', *NBER Working Paper*, No. 3920, (November).

Coakley, Jerry and Laurence Harris (1994), 'Financial Globalisation and Deregulation' in J. Michie, (ed), *The Economic Legacy: 1979-1992*, London: Academic Press.

Cohen, G.D. and J. Wenninger (1994), 'Changing Relationship Between the Spread and the Funds Rate', *Federal Reserve Bank of New York Working Paper* No. 9408, (May).

Cook, T. and T. Hahn (1989), 'The Effects of Changes in the Federal Funds Rate Target on Market Interest Rates in the 1970s', *Journal of Monetary Economics*, (November), pp. 331-335.

Corbett, J. (1987), 'International Perspectives on Financing: Evidence from Japan', *Oxford Review of Economic Policy*, **3** (4), pp. 30-55.

Corbettt, J. (1990), 'Policy Issues in the Design of Banking', *European Economy*, **42**, pp. 205-215.

Corbettt, J. and T. Jenkinson (1994), 'The Financing of Industry, 1970-1989: An International Comparison', *Centre for Economic Policy Research* Discussion Paper No. 948.

Corbett, J. and T. Jenkinson (1996), 'The Financing of Industry, 1970-1989: An International Comparison', *Journal of the Japanese and International Economies*, **10**, pp. 71-96.

Cosh, Andrew, Alan Hughes, and Ajit Singh, (1992), 'Openness, Financial Innovation, Changing Patterns of Ownership, and the Structure of

Financial Markets', in A. Banuri and J. Schor (eds), *Financial Openness and National Autonomy*, Oxford: Clarendon Press.

Cox, Andrew (1986), 'The State, Finance and Industry Relationship in Comparative Perspective', in A. Cox (ed.), *The State, Finance, and Industry*, Sussex: Wheatsheaf Books, pp. 1-59.

Crotty, James and Don Goldstein (1993), 'Do US Financial Markets Allocate Credit Efficiently? The Case of Corporate Restructuring in the 1980s', in G. Dymski, G. Epstein, and R. Pollin (eds), *Transforming the US Financial System: Equity and Efficiency for the 21 st Century*, Armonk: ME Sharpe.

Cumby, R.E. and F.S. Mishkin (1986), 'The international Linkage of Real Interest Rates: The European- US Connection', *Journal of International Money and Finance*, 5 (March), pp.5-23.

Cumby, R.E. and M. Obstfeld, (1984), 'International Interest Rate and Price Level Linkages under Flexible Exchange Rates', in J.F. Bilson, and R.C. Marston (eds), *Exchange Rate Theory and Practice*, Chicago: University of Chicago Press.

Cumming, Christine M. and Lawrence M. Sweet (1988), 'Financial Structure of the G-10 Countries: How Does the United States Compare?', *Federal Reserve Bank of New York Quarterly Review*, (Winter), pp. 14-25.

Cummins, J.G., K.A. Hassett, and R.G. Hubbard (1994), 'A Reconsideration of Investment Behaviour Using Tax Reforms as Natural Experiments', *Brookings Papers on Economic Activity*, 2, pp. 1-74.

D'Arista, Jane and Tom Schlesinger, (1993), 'The Parallel Banking System', in G. Dymski, G. Epstein and R. Pollin (eds), *Transforming the US Financial System: Equity and Efficiency for the 21ˢᵗ Century*, Armonk: M.E. Sharpe.

Davidson, Paul (1972), *Money and the Real World*, London: Macmillan.

Devereux, M.P. and F. Schiantarelli (1990), 'Investment, Financial Factors and Cash Flow from UK Panel Data', in R.G. Hubbard (ed.), *Information, Capital Market and Investment*, Chicago: University of Chicago Press.

Dooley, Michael, Jeffrey Frankel, and Donald J. Mathieson (1987), 'International Capital Mobility: What Do Saving-Investment Correlations Tell Us?', *International Monetary Fund Staff Papers*, 34, pp. 503-530.

Dooley, M., and P. Isard (1980), 'Capital Controls, Political Risk, and Deviations from Interest-Rate Parity', *Journal of Political Economy*, 88 (2), pp. 370-384

Dornbusch, Rudiger and Alberto Giovannini (1990), 'Monetary Policy in the Open Economy', in Benjamin Friedman and Frank Hahn (eds), *Handbook of Monetary Economics Vol. II*, Amsterdam: Elsevier Science, pp. 1231-1303.

Dreze, J. and F. Modigliani (1972), 'Consumption Under Uncertainty', *Journal of Economic Theory*, **5**, pp. 308-335.

Edwards, Jeremy and Klaus Fischer (1994), *Banks, Finance and Investment in Germany*, Cambridge: Cambridge University Press.

Eichenbaum, Martin and Evans, Charles (1993), 'Some Empirical Evidence on the Effects of Monetary Policy Shocks on Exchange Rates', *NBER Working Paper* No. 4271.

Elston, J.A., and H. Albach (1995), 'Firm Ownership Structure and Investment: Evidence from German Manufacturing', *IFO Studien Zeitschrift fur Empiriische Wirtschaftsforschung*, Heft 1.

Elton, Edwin J. and Martin J. Gruber (1990), *Japanese Capital Markets*, New York: Harper & Row.

Epstein, Gerald (1993), 'Monetary Policy in the 1990s: Overcoming the Barriers to Equity and Growth', in G. Dymski, G.Epstein, and R. Pollin (eds), *Transforming the U.S. Financial System: Equity and Efficiency for the 21st Century*, Armonk: M.E. Sharpe, pp. 65-100.

Epstein, Gerald and Juliet Schor (1992), 'Structural Determinants and Economic Effects of Capital Controls in OECD Countries', in A. Banuri and J. Schor (eds), *Financial Openness and National Autonomy*, Oxford: Clarendon Press, pp. 136-62.

Estrella, Arturo and Gikas Hardouvelis (1990), 'Possible Roles of the Yield Curve in Monetary Policy', in Federal Reserve Bank of New York, *Intermediate Targets and Indicators for Monetary Policy: A Critical Survey*, pp. 339-362.

Fama, E. (1984), 'Forward and Spot Exchange Rates,' *Journal of Monetary Economics*, **14**, pp. 319-338.

Fazzari, Steven (1993), 'Monetary Policy, Financial Structure and Investment', in G. Dymski, G. Epstein and R. Pollin (eds), *Transforming the U.S. Financial System: Equity and Efficiency for the 21st Century*, Armonk: M.E. Sharpe.

Fazzari, Steven and Michael Athey (1987), 'Asymmetric Information, Financing Constraints, and Investment', *Review of Economics and Statistics*, **69**, pp. 481-487.

Fazzari, S. and T. Mott (1986) 'The Investment Theories of Kalecki and Keynes: An Empirical Study of Firm Data, 1970-82', *Journal of Post Keynesian Economics*, **9** (Winter), pp. 171-187.

Fazzari, S., G. Hubbard and B. Petersen (1988), 'Financing Constraints and Corporate Investment', *Brookings Papers on Economic Activity*, **1**, pp. 141-195.

Feldstein, M. and C. Horioka (1980), 'Domestic Saving and International Capital Flows', *Economic Journal*, **90**, pp. 314-329.

Frankel, A. and J. Montgomery (1991), 'Financial Structure: An International perspective', *Brookings Papers on Economic Activity*, **1**, pp. 257-297.

Frankel, Jeffrey (1990), 'International Financial Integration, Relations among Interest Rates and Exchange Rates, and Monetary Indicators', in C. Pigott (ed.), *International Financial Integration and US Monetary Policy*, New York: Federal Reserve Bank of New York.

Frankel, J. (1992), 'Measuring International Capital Mobility: A Review', *American Economic Review*, **82** (2), pp. 197-202.

Frankel, Jeffrey and K Froot, (1990), 'Exchange Rate Forecasting Techniques, Survey Data, and Implications for the Foreign Exchange Market', *NBER Working paper* No. *3470*

Frenkel, J. and R. Levich (1975), 'Covered Interest Arbitrage: Unexploited Profits?', *Journal of Political Economy*, **83** (2), pp.325-338.

Frieden, J. (1991), 'Invested Interests: The Politics of National Economic Policies in a World of Global Finance', *International Organization*, **45** (4).

Friedman, Benjamin (1989), 'Changing Effects of Monetary Policy on Real Economic Activity', in *Monetary Policy Issues in the 1990s*, Federal Reserve Bank of Kansas City.

Friedman, Benjamin and Kenneth Kuttner (1992), 'Money, Income, Prices, and Interest Rates', *American Economic Review*, **82** (3), pp. 472-492.

Friedman, Milton (1957), *A Theory of the Consumption Function*, Princeton: Princeton University Press.

Froot, K.A. and J.A. Frankel (1989), 'Forward Discount Bias: Is it an Exchange Rate Premium?', *Quarterly Journal of Economics*, **104**, pp. 139-161.

Gardener, Edward M. and Philip Molyneux (1990), *Changes in Western European Banking*, London: Unwin Hyman.

Gerschenkron, Alexander (1962), *Economic Backwardness in Historical Perspective*, Cambridge: The Belknap Press of Harvard University.

Gertler, M. and S. Gilchrist (1994), 'Monetary Policy, Business Cycles and the Behaviour of Small Manufacturing Firms', *Quarterly Journal of Economics*, **109**, pp. 309-340.

Gertler, Mark and R. Glen Hubbard (1988), 'Financial Factors in Business Fluctuations', in *Financial Market Volatility: Causes, Consequences, and Policy Recommendations*, Federal Reserve Bank of Kansas City.

Gertner, R. and D. Scharfstein (1990), 'A Theory of Workouts and the Effects of Reorganization Law', *Journal of Finance*, **46**(1), pp. 189-222.

Glyn, Andrew (1992), 'Exchange Controls and Policy Autonomy: The Case of Australia, 1983-1988', in A. Banuri and J. Schor (eds), *Financial Openness and National Autonomy*, Oxford: Clarendon Press, pp. 110-135.

Goldsmith, Raymond W. (1969), *Financial Structure and Development*, New Haven: Yale University Press.

Goldstein, Don (1995), 'Financial Structure and Corporate Behaviour in Japan and the US: Insulation vs. Integration with Speculative Pressures', Working Paper, University of Massachusetts, Amherst.

Goodman, John B. (1992), *Monetary Sovereignty: The Politics of Central Banking in Western Europe*, Ithaca: Cornell University Press.

Goodman, J.B. and L.W. Pauly (1993), 'The Obsolescence of Capital Controls? Economic Management in an Age of Global Markets', *World Politics*, **46**, pp. 50-82.

Goodfriend, Marvin (1991), 'Interest Rates and the Conduct of Monetary Policy', in A.H. Meltzer and C.I. Plosser (eds), *Carnegie–Rochester Conference Series on Public Policy*, **34** (Spring), pp. 7-30.

Grabel, Ilene (1997), '*Saving and the Financing of Productive Investment: The Importance of National Financial Complexes*', in R. Pollin (ed.), *The Macroeconomics of Finance, Saving and Investment*. Ann Arbor: University of Michigan Press.

Granger, C. (1981), 'Some Properties of Time Series Data and Their Use in Econometric Model Specification', *Journal of Econometrics*, **16**, pp. 121-130.

Greenwald, Bruce and Joseph Stiglitz (1988) 'Examining Alternative Macroeconomic Theories,' *Brookings Papers on Economic Activity*, **1**, pp. 207-268.

Greenwald, Bruce and Joseph Stiglitz (1990), 'Macroeconomic Models with Equity and Credit Rationing', in R. Glenn Hubbard (ed.), *Asymmetric Information, Corporate Finance, and Investment*, Chicago: University of Chicago Press, pp. 15-43.

Greenwald, Bruce and Joseph Stiglitz (1991), 'Towards a Reformulation of Monetary Theory: Competitive Banking', *The Economic and Social Review*, **23** (1), pp.1-34.

Gurley, J. and E. Shaw (1955), 'Financial Aspects of Economic Development', *American Economic Review*, **45** (4), pp. 515-538.

Haq, Mahbub ul, Inge Kaul, and Isabelle Grunberg (1996), *The Tobin Tax: Coping with Financial Volatility*, Oxford: Oxford University Press.

Hardouvelis, G.A. (1994), 'The Term Structure Spread and Future Changes in Long and Short Rates in the G-7 Countries: Is There a Puzzle?', *Journal of Monetary Economics*, (April), pp. 255-283.

Harris, Laurence (1988), 'Alternative Perspectives on the Financial System', in L. Harris, J. Coakley, M. Croasdale, and T. Evans (eds), *New Perspectives on the Financial System*, New York: M.E. Sharpe.

Hawley, James P. (1987), *Dollars & Borders: U.S. Government Attempts to Restrict Capital Flows, 1960- 1980*, New York: M.E. Sharpe.

Helleiner, E. (1994), 'Freeing Money: Why Have States Been More Willing to Liberalize Capital Controls than Trade Barriers', *Policy Sciences*, **27**, pp. 299-318.

Henning, Randall C. (1994), *Currencies and politics in the United States, Germany, and Japan*, Washington, D.C.: Institute for International Economics.

Herring, Richard J. and Robert E Litan (1995), *Financial Regulation in the Global Economy*, Washington, D.C: The Brookings Institution.

Hilferding, Rudolph (1910), *Finance Capital: A Study of the Latest Phase of Capitalist Development*, London: Routledge & Kegan Paul.

Hirtle, Beverley and Jeanette Kelleher (1990), 'Financial Market Evolution and the Interest Sensitivity of Output', *Federal Reserve Bank of New York Quarterly Review*, (Summer), pp.105-123.

Hirschman, Albert (1970), *Exit, Voice, and Loyalty: Responses to Decline in Firms, Organizations, and States*, Cambridge: Harvard University Press.

Hodder, James (1988), 'Corporate Capital Structure in the United States and Japan: Financial Intermediation and Implications of Financial Deregulation', in J. Shoven, (ed.), *Government Policy Towards Industry in the United States and Japan*, Cambridge: Cambridge University Press, pp. 241-264.

Hoshi, Takeo (1994), 'The Economic Role of Corporate Grouping and the Main Bank System', in H. Aoki and M. Dore (eds), *The Japanese Firm*, Oxford: Oxford University Press.

Hoshi, T., A. Kashyap, and D. Scharfstein (1990), 'The Role of Banks in Reducing the Cost of Financial Distress in Japan', *Journal of Financial Economics*, **67**.

Icard, A. (1994), 'The Transmission of Monetary Policy in France', *Journal of Monetary Economics*, **33** (1), pp. 87-103.

Inoue, Y. (1989), 'Globalization of Business Finance', *Japanese Economic Studies*, **17** (4), pp.41- 91.

International Monetary Fund (1993), *International Financial Statistics*, Washington DC: International Monetary Fund.

Jacobs, Michael P. (1994), 'A Cluster Analysis of Twelve Countries' Financial Systems', Essay I, Ph.D. Dissertation, New School for Social Research.

Jensen, Michael C. (1991), 'Corporate Control and the Politics of Finance', *Journal of Applied Corporate Finance*, **12**, pp.62-80.

Jensen, M. and W. Meckling (1976), 'The Theory of the Firm: Managerial Behaviour, Agency Costs, and Ownership Structure', *Journal of Financial Economics*, **3**, pp. 305-360.

Kahn, George A. (1989), 'The Changing Interest Sensitivity of the US Economy', *Federal Reserve Bank of Kansas City Economic Review*, (November), pp. 13-33.

Kalecki, M. (1937), 'The Principle of Increasing Risk,' *Economica*, **4**, (November), pp. 440-447.

Kashyap, A., O. Lamont and J. Stein (1994), 'Credit Conditions and the Cyclical Behaviour of Inventories', *The Quarterly Journal of Economics*, (August), pp.565-592.

Kashyap, A. and J. Stein (1995), 'The Impact of Monetary Policy on Bank Balance Sheets', *Carnegie–Rochester Conference Series on Public Policy*, **42**, pp. 151-195.

Kashyap, A., J. Stein and D. Wilcox (1993), 'Monetary Policy and Credit Conditions: Evidence from the Composition of External Finance', *American Economic Review*, **83** (1), pp. 78-98.

Kasman, B. (1992), 'A Comparison of Monetary Policy Operating Procedures in Six Industrial Coutries', *Federal Reserve Bank of New York Quarterly Review*, (Summer), pp. 5-24.

Kasman, B. and C. Pigott (1988), 'Interest Rate Divergences Among the Major Industrial Nations', *Federal Reserve Bank of New York Quarterly Review*, (Autumn), pp. 28-44.

Kasman, B. and A. Rodrigues (1991), 'Financial Liberalization and Monetary Control in Japan', *Federal Reserve Bank of New York Quarterly Review*, (Autumn), pp. 28-45.

Kaufman, George G. (1992), *Banking Structures in Major Countries*, Boston: Kluwer Academic Publishers.

Keynes, John M. (1936), *The General Theory of Employment, Interest, and Money*, London: Macmillan.

King, Mervyn (1990), 'International Harmonisation of the Regulation of Capital Markets: An Introduction', *European Economic Review*, **34**, pp. 569-577.

Koechlin, Timothy (1992), 'The Responsiveness of Domestic Investment to Foreign Economic Conditions', *Journal of Post Keynesian Economics,* **15** (1), pp. 63-84.

Kregel, J.A. (1993), 'Bank Supervision: The Real Hurdle to European Monetary Union', *Journal of Economic Issues,* **27** (2), pp. 667-677.

Lee, Simon (1996), 'Finance for Industry', in J. Michie and J. Grieve Smith (eds), *Creating Industrial Capacity: Towards Full Employment,* Oxford: Oxford University Press.

Leeper, E.M. and D.B. Gordon (1992), 'In Search of the Liquidity Effect', *Journal of Monetary Economics,* (June), pp. 341-369.

Leland, H. (1968), 'Saving and Uncertainty: The Precautionary Demand for Saving, *Quarterly Journal of Economics,* **82,** pp. 465-473.

Levich, Richard M. (1985), 'Empirical Studies of Exchange Rates: Price Behaviour, Rate Determination, and Market Efficiency', in Jones and Kenan (eds), *Handbook of International Economics Vol. II,* Amsterdam: North-Holland.

Ley, R. (1989), 'Liberating Capital Movements: A New OECD Commitment', *OECD Observer,* **159** (August–September), pp. 22-26.

Loriaux, Michael (1991), *France After Hegemony,* Ithaca: Cornell University Press.

Loriaux, Michael (1997), 'Socialist Monetarism and Financial Liberlization in France', in Loriaux et al. (eds), *Capital Ungoverned: Liberalizing Finance in Interventionist States,* Ithaca: Cornell University Press.

MacDonald, Robert (1988), *Floating Exchange Rates: Theories and Evidence,* London: Unwin Hyman.

MacDonald, R. and M.P. Taylor (1989), 'International Parity Conditions', *Greek Economic Review,* **11,** pp. 257-290.

MacEwan, Arthur (1991), 'What's New About the "New International Economy"?', *Socialist Review,* **21,** pp. 3-4.

Mahdavi, S., A. Sohrabian, and S. Kholdy (1994), 'Cointegration and Error Correction Models: The Temporal Causality Between Investment and Corporate Cash Flow', *Journal of Post-Keynesian Economics,* **16** (3), pp. 478-99.

Maisel, Sherman (1973), 'Improving Our System of Credit Allocation', in Federal Reserve Bank of Boston, *Credit Allocation Techniques and Monetary Policy,* pp. 15-30.

Mankiw, N.G. (1986), 'The Term Structure of Interest Rates Revisited', *Brookings Papers on Economic Activity,* **1,** pp. 61-96.

Marx, Karl (1981), *Capital: Volume III,* New York: Vintage.

Mauskopf, E. (1990), 'The Transmission Channels of Monetary Policy: How Have They Changed?', *Federal Reserve Bulletin,* (December).

Mayer, C. (1987), 'Financial Systems and Corporate Investment', *Oxford Review of Economic Policy*, **3**, pp. i-xvi.

Mayer, C. (1988), 'New Issues in Corporate Finance', *European Economic Review*, **32**, pp. 1167- 1189.

Mayer, Colin (1990), 'Financial Systems, Corporate Finance, and Economic Development', in R.G. Hubbard (ed.), *Asymmetric Information, Corporate Finance, and Investment*, Chicago: University of Chicago Press.

Mayer, Colin (1994), 'The Assessment: Money and Banking: Theory and Evidence', *Oxford Review of Economic Policy*, **10** (4), pp. 1-13.

Mayer, Colin and Ian Alexander (1990), 'Banks and Securities Markets: Corporate Financing in Germany and the United Kingdom', *Journal of the Japanese and International Economies*, **4**, pp. 450-475.

McCallum, B.T. (1994), 'A Reconsideration of the Uncovered Interest Parity Relationship', *Journal of Monetary Economics*, **33**, November., pp. 105-132.

McCauley, R.N, and S. Rama (1992), 'Foreign Bank Credit to US Corporations: The Implications of Offshore Loans', *Federal Reserve Bank of New York Quarterly Review*, (Spring), pp. 52-65.

McCauley, R.N. and S.A. Zimmer (1989), 'Explaining International Differences in the Cost of Capital', *New York Federal Reserve Bank Quarterly Review*, (Summer), pp. 7-28.

Melitz, Jacques (1990), 'Financial Deregulation in France', *European Economic Review*, **34**, pp. 394- 402.

Minsky, Hyman (1975), *John Maynard Keynes*, New York: Columbia University Press.

Minsky, Hyman (1986), *Stabilizing an Unstable Economy*, New Haven: Yale University Press.

Mishkin, F. (1984), 'Are Real Interest Rates Equal Across Countries? An Empirical Investigation of International Parity Conditions', *Journal of Finance*, **39**, pp. 1345-1358.

Modjtahedi, B (1987), 'An Empirical Investigation Into the International Real Interest Rates Linkage', *Canadian Journal of Economics*, **20** (November).

Moran, Michael (1991), *The Politics of the Financial Services Revolution*, London: Macmillan.

Mosser, Patricia (1992), 'Changes in Monetary Policy Effectiveness: Evidence from Large Macroeconometric Models', *Federal Reserve Bank of New York Quarterly Review*, (Spring), pp. 36-51.

Mott, Tracy L. (1982), 'Kalecki's Principle of Increasing Risk: The Role of Finance in the Post-Keynesian Theory of Investment Fluctuations', Ph.D. Dissertation, Stanford University.

Murphy, R. (1984), 'Capital Mobility and the Relationship between Saving and Investment in OECD Countries', *Journal of International Money and Finance*, **3**, pp. 327-342.

Myers, S. (1977), 'The Determinants of Corporate Borrowing', *Journal of Financial Economics*, **5**, pp. 147-175.

Neal, Larry (1990), *The Rise of Financial Capitalism: Internationl Capital Markets in the Age of Reason*, Cambridge: Cambridge University Press.

O'Brien, Richard (1992), *Global Financial Integration: The End of Geography*, New York: Council on Foreign Relations.

OECD (1987), *OECD Economic Surveys: France*, Paris: OECD.

OECD (1989), *OECD Economic Surveys: Japan*, Paris: OECD.

Pauly, L.W. (1994), 'National Financial Structure, Capital Mobility, and International Economic Rules: The Normative Consequences of East Asian, European, and American Distinctiveness', *Policy Sciences*, **27**, pp. 343-360

Perry, G. and Charles Schultze (1993), 'Was this Recession Different? Are they all Different?', *Brookings Papers on Economic Activity*, **1**, pp. 145-195.

Petersen, M. and R. Rajan, (1994), 'The Benefits of Lending Relationships: Evidence from Small Business Data', *The Journal of Finance*, **49** (1), pp. 3-37.

Pollin, R. (1991), 'Two Theories of Money Supply Endogeneity: Some Empirical Evidence', *Journal of Post Keynesian Economics*, **13** (3).

Pollin, Robert (1993), 'Public Credit Allocation through the Federal Reserve: Why It Is Needed; How It Should Be Done,' in G. Dymski, G. Epstein, and R. Pollin (eds), *Transforming the U.S. Financial System: Equity and Efficiency for the 21st Century*, Armonk: M.E. Sharpe, pp. 321-354.

Pollin, Robert (1994), 'Borrowing More but Investing Less: Economic Stagnation and the Rise of Corporate Takeovers in the US', Manuscript, University of California-Riverside, Department of Economics.

Pollin, R. (1995), 'Financial Structures and Egalitarian Economic Policy', *New Left Review*, (214).

Pollin, R. and M. Schaberg, (1998), 'Asset Exchanges, Financial Market Trading and the M1 Income Velocity Puzzle', *Journal of Post Keynesian Economics*.

Poole, William (1991), 'Interest Rates and the Conduct of Monetary Policy: A Comment', in A.H. Meltzer and C.I. Plosser (eds), *Carnegie-Rochester Conference Series on Public Policy*, **34**, (Spring), pp. 31-39.

Porter, Michael (1992), *Capital Choices: Changing the Way America Invests in Industry*, Washington D.C.: Council on Competitiveness.

Porter, Tony (1993), *States, Markets, and Regimes in Global Finance*, New York: St. Martin's Press

Poterba, James and Lawrence Summers (1992), 'Time Horizons of American Firms: New Evidence from a Survey of CEOs', manuscript, Department of Economics, Massachusetts Institute of Technology.

Pozdena R and J. Alexander (1992), 'Tax Policy and Corporate Capital Structure', Federal Reserve Bank of San Francisco Economic Review, **4**, pp. 37-51.

Prowse, S. (1990), 'Institutional Investment Patterns and Corporate Financial Behaviour in the United States and Japan,' *Journal of Financial Economics*, **27**, pp. 43-66.

Radecki, L. and V. Reinhart (1988), 'The Globalization of Financial Markets and the Effectiveness of Monetary Policy Instruments', *Federal Reserve Bank of New York Quarterly Review*, (Autumn), pp. 18-27.

Radecki, Lawrence J. and Vincent Reinhart (1994), 'The Financial Linkages in the Transmission of Monetary Policy in the United States', in Bank for International Settlements, *National Differences in Interest Rate Transmission*, Basle: Bank for International Settlements, pp. 291-337.

Radice, H. (1984), 'The National Economy: A Keynesian Myth?', *Capital and Class*, **22** (Spring), pp.111- 140.

Raymond, Robert (1992), 'The Effects of Financial Innovation and Deregulation on French Monetary Policy', in S. Frowen and D. Kath (eds), *Monetary Policy and Financial Innovations in Five Industrial Countries*, New York: St. Martin's Press, pp. 82-101.

Resnick, B. (1989), 'The Globalization of World Financial Markets', *Business Horizon*, (November–December).

Roe, Mark J. (1996), 'The Voting Prohibition in Bond Workouts, in J. Bhandari and L. Weiss (eds), *Corporate Bankruptcy*, Cambridge: Cambridge University Press, pp. 415-434.

Rybczynski, T. (1984), 'Industrial Finance System in Europe, U.S. and Japan', *Journal of Economic Behaviour and Organization*, **5**, pp. 275-286.

Rybczynski, T. (1985), 'Financial Systems, Risk and Public Policy', *The Royal Bank of Scotland Review*, **16** (4), pp.35-45.

Sandmo, A., (1972) The Effect of Uncertainty on Savings Decisions,' *Review of Economic Studies*, **37**, pp. 82-114.

Sarver, Eugene (1990), *The Eurocurrency Market Handbook*, New York: New York Institute of Finance.

Schaberg, Marc (1997), 'National Financial Systems, Globalization, and Investment: A Cross-Country Analysis', Ph.D. Dissertation, University of California–Riverside.

Schaller, H. (1993), 'Asymmetric Information, Liquidity Constraints, and Canadian Investment',*Canadian Journal of Economics*, **26**, pp. 552-574.

Schiantarelli, F. and A. Sembenelli (1995), 'Form of Ownership and Financial Constraints: Panel Data Evidence from Leverage and Investment Equations', Mimeo, Boston College.

Schor, Juliet (1992), 'Introduction', in A. Banuri and J. Schor (eds), *Financial Openness and National Autonomy*, Oxford: Clarendon Press, pp. 1-15.

Schumpeter, Joseph (1912), *The Theory of Economic Development*. Cambridge: Harvard University Press.

Sheard, Paul (1985), 'Main Banks and Structural Adjustment in Japan', Research Paper No. 129, Austrailia-Japan Research Centre.

Sheard, Paul (1992), 'The Role of the Japanese Main Bank when Borrowing Firms are in Financial Distress', *Center for Economic Policy Research Publications No. 330*, Stanford University.

Smith, Roy C. and Ingo Walter (1991), 'Reconfiguration of Global Financial Markets in the 1990s,' in R. O'Brien and S. Hewin (eds), *Finance and the International Economy: The Amex Bank Review Prize Essay*, Oxford: Oxford University Press, pp. 142-168.

Stiglitz, Joseph E. (1992a), 'Banks vs. Markets as Mechanisms for Allocating and Coordinating Investment', in J.A. Roumasset and S. Barr (eds), *The Economics of Cooperation: East Asian Development and the Case for Pro-Market Intervention*, Boulder: Westview Press, pp. 15-38.

Stiglitz, J.E. (1992b), 'Capital Markets and Economic Fluctuations in Capitalist Countries', *European Economic Review*, **36**, pp. 269-306.

Stiglitz, Joseph E. (1993), 'The Role of the State in Financial Markets', Manuscript, Department of Economics, Stanford University.

Suzuki, S. and R. Wright (1985), 'Financial Structure and Bankruptcy Risk in Japanese Companies,' *Journal of International Business Studies*, pp. 97-110.

Tobin, James and William Brainard (1963), 'Financial Intermediaries and the Effectiveness of Monetary Control,' *American Economic Review*, **53** (3), pp. 383-400.

Wallich, H.C. (1985), 'U.S. Monetary Policy in an Interdependent World', in W.J. Ethier and R.C. Marston, (eds), *International Financial Markets and Capital Movements: A Symposium in Honor of Arthur I.*

Bloomfield, Princeton University. International Finance Section, Essays in International Finance, (157).

White, Michelle (1996), 'The Costs of Corporate Bankruptcy: A US–European Comparison,' in J. Bhandari and L. Weiss eds, *Corporate Bankruptcy: Economic and Legal Perspectives*, Cambridge: Cambridge University Press, pp. 467-500.

Whited, T. (1992), 'Debt, Liquidity Constraints, and Corporate Investment: Evidence from Panel Data', *Journal of Finance,* **47**(4), pp. 1425-1460.

Ye, Than (1992), *Globalization of Financial Markets: Its Impact on the SEACAN Countries*, Kuala Lumpur: The South East Asian Central Banks Research and Training Centre.

Zeldes, S.P (1989), 'Optimal Consumption With Stochastic Income: Deviations from Certainty Equivalence,' *Quarterly Journal of Economics,* **104**, pp. 275-298.

Zevin, Robert (1992), 'Are World Financial Markets More Open? If So, Why and with What Effects?' in A Banuri and J. Schor (eds), *Financial Openness and National Autonomy*, Oxford: Clarendon Press.

Zysman, John (1983), *Governments, Markets, and Growth*, Ithaca:Cornell University Press.

Index

accounting data
  use for comparisons 8

bank-based financial systems *see*
  voice-dominated financial systems
bank finance
  and investment 76-7
  relationship with internal funds 65, 71,
    75-6
  share of sources of funds 114-16, 121,
    125
  volatility 63, 64, 65
  see also ready funds
Banking Act 1984 (France) 41-2
bankruptcy
  risk of 52
banks
  close ties with 52-4, 55, 57-8, 98-9
  see also bank finance;
    voice-dominated financial
    systems
borrower's risk 49
  effect on investment 55-6
  elements of 51, 52
  influence of institutional arrangements
    51-4

capital
  cost of 13
  removal of controls 106
cash flow *see* internal funds
close bank ties 52-4, 55, 57-8, 98-9
closed interest rate parity 108
co-ordination 12
company accounting data
  use for comparisons 8
convergence 111-13
  France 101-2
  monetary policy 145, 146
  sources of funds 113-17, 121, 125
  uses of funds 125-6, 129, 132

see also European Monetary Union
cost of capital 13
covered interest rate parity 108
credit
  control of 137, 138, 141, 146-8,
    153-4
  see also lending channel

data sources 9
'debt overhang' 55
default risk 51-2
demand price 48, 49, 50
deregulation of financial markets 105-6,
  107
directed lending 137-8

EMU 148-9
equities *see* financial assets purchases
Euromarkets 107
European Monetary Union (EMU)
  148-9
exit-dominated financial systems
  bank finance / investment relationship
    77
  cash flow / investment relationship 99,
    100
  financial assets purchases 82
  investment
    financing of 56-8, 71
    levels of 101
    volatility 83, 84, 101
  liquidity 58-61
  ready funds / investment relationship 97,
    98
  ready funds volatility 72, 73
  sources of funds / investment
    relationship 84, 90, 91
  uses of funds 16, 19, 23-4, 81

financial assets purchases
  France 82-3, 154-5

precautionary motives 81, 82
  share of gross sources of funds 16, 18
  share of uses of funds 126, 129, 132
  speculative motives 82, 154, 155, 156
  see also liquidity
financial distress 52
flow of funds data
  sources 8
  use for comparisons 8, 9–11
foreign exchange control
  Japan 147
France
  bank finance
    share of total sources 115–16, 117,
      135
    volatility 64
  bank finance / internal funds
    relationship 65, 71, 75, 76
  Banking Act (1984) 41–2
  convergence towards exit-dominated
    system 101–2
  credit control 147–8
  financial asset purchases 82–3, 154–5
    share of gross sources of funds 16
    share of uses of funds 126, 129, 132
  gross sources of funds 21–2, 39, 42
  internal funds
    share of total sources 115, 116, 117
    volatility 64
  investment volatility 83–4
  levels of investment 78, 80
  net sources of funds 20–1, 39, 41
  physical investment
    share of gross sources of funds 16,
      19
    share of uses of funds 125–6
  ready funds / investment relationship
    91, 97
  ready funds volatility 72, 73
  reserve requirements 151–2
  sources of funds / investment
    relationship 90, 91
  uses of funds 22–4, 42–3

Germany
  bank finance
    share of total sources 116, 117
    volatility 64
  bank finance / internal funds
    relationship 65, 71, 75, 76

financial assets purchases
  share of gross sources of funds 16
  share of uses of funds 126, 129, 132
gross sources of finance 21–2, 35, 37
internal funds
  share of total sources 115, 116,
    117
  volatility 64
investment volatility 83–4
levels of investment 78
net sources of funds 20–21, 35, 37
physical investment
  share of gross sources of funds
    16
  share of uses of funds 125–6
ready funds / investment
  relationship 91, 97
ready funds volatility 72
reserve requirements 152
sources of funds / investment
  relationship 90, 91
uses of funds 22–4, 38, 39
gross sources of funds 21–2
  calculation of 10
  convergence 113–17, 121, 125
  France 39, 42
  Germany 35, 37
  Japan 31, 33–4
  relationship with investment 84, 90,
    91
  UK 29–30
  US 24, 45
  see also bank finance; internal
    funds
guided lending 137–8

IBFs (US) 107
incentive compatability 11, 12
integration 110–11
  price measures of 108–10
  quantity measures of 107
interest rate controls 137, 141–3
interest rate parity 108–10
internal funds
  and investment 55–8, 98–100
  relationship with bank finance 65, 71,
    75–6
  share of sources of funds 114–17, 121,
    125
  volatility 64

see also ready funds
International Banking Facilities (IBFs)
(US) 107
investment
and bank finance 76-7
borrower's risk 49, 51-6
and cash flow 55-8, 98-100
demand price 48, 49, 50
lender's risk 48, 49, 54-6
levels of 78, 80, 101
physical 10
share of gross sources of funds 16,
19
share of uses of funds 125-6, 129
productive
promoting 139, 155-6
and ready funds 91, 97-8
and sources of funds 84, 90, 91
supply price 49, 50
two-price model 49-50
volatility 83-4, 101

Japan
bank finance
share of total sources 115-16, 117
volatility 64
bank finance / internal funds
relationship 65, 71, 75, 76
bank finance / investment relationship
76-7
credit control
dismantling of 146-7
financial assets purchases
share of gross sources of funds 16
share of uses of funds 126, 129, 132
foreign exchange control 147
gross sources of funds 21-2, 31, 33-4
internal funds
share of total sources 115, 116, 117
volatility 64
investment volatility 83-4
levels of investment 78
net sources of funds 20-21, 31, 33
physical investment
share of gross sources of funds 16
share of uses of funds 125-6
ready funds / investment relationship
91, 97
ready funds volatility 72
sources of funds / investment

relationship 90
uses of funds 22-4, 34-5

lender's risk 48, 49, 54-6
lending channel 143-5, 150-52
liquidity
impact of institutional arrangements
58-61
literature
financial systems 1-7
long-term financing
voice-dominated financial systems 12

methodology 9-11
monetary policy
control of interest rates 141-3
convergence 145, 146
direct instruments 137-8
effectiveness 138, 141, 145, 153
indirect instruments 138, 145, 146,
150, 153-4
lending channel 143-5, 150-52

net sources of funds 20-21
calculation of 10
convergence 114-17, 121, 125
France 41
Germany 35, 37
Japan 31, 33
UK 27, 29
US 24, 26-7
see also bank finance; internal funds
non-bank intermediaries
regulations 139

precautionary motives
financial assets purchases 81, 82
preferred assets 153-4
price measures of integration 108-10
principal - agent problem
incentive compatability 11, 12
productive investment
promoting 139, 155-6

quantity measures of integration 107

ready funds
and investment 91, 97-8
volatility 72-3
see also bank finance; internal funds

real interest rate parity 109–10
regulations
  non–bank intermediaries 139
reserve requirements 150–52, 153–4
risk
  borrower's 49, 51–6
  lender's 48, 49, 54–6

securities transaction tax 155–6
'short-termism' 12
  easing problem of 139, 155
sources of funds
  gross *see* gross sources of funds
  net *see* net sources of funds
speculative motives
  financial assets purchases 82, 154,
    155, 156
stock and bond purchases (SBP) *see*
    financial assets purchases
supply price 49, 50

tax on financial transactions 155–6
'Tobin Tax' 155
two-price model of investment 49–50

uncovered interest rate parity 108–9
United Kingdom (UK)
  bank finance
    volatility 64
  bank finance / internal funds
    relationship 65, 71, 75, 76
  financial assets purchases
    share of gross sources of funds 16
    share of uses of funds 126, 129,
      132
  gross sources of funds 21–2, 29–30
  internal funds
    share of total sources 115
    volatility 72
  investment volatility 83–4
  levels of investment 78
  net sources of funds 20–21, 27, 29
  physical investment
    share of gross sources of funds 16,
      19
    share of uses of funds 125–6
  ready funds / investment relationship
    91, 97
  ready funds volatility 72
  sources of funds / investment

    relationship 90, 91
  uses of funds 22–4, 30–1
United States (US)
  bank finance
    volatility 64
  bank finance / internal funds
    relationship 65, 71, 75, 76
  financial assets purchases
    share of gross sources of funds 16
    share of uses of funds 126, 129, 132
  gross sources of funds 21–2, 24, 45
  internal funds
    share of total sources 115
    volatility 64
  International Banking Facilities 107
  investment volatility 83–4
  levels of investment 78
  net sources of funds 20–21, 24, 26–7
  physical investment
    share of gross sources of funds 16,
      19
    share of uses of funds 125–6
  ready funds / investment relationship
    91, 97
  ready funds volatility 72
  sources of funds / investment
    relationship 90, 91
  uses of funds 22–4, 27
  uses of funds 22–4
    convergence 125–6, 129, 132
    exit-dominated financial systems
      16, 19, 23–4, 81
    France 42–3
    Germany 38, 39
    Japan 34–5
    measuring 15–16
    types of 15
    UK 30–31
    US 27
    voice-dominated financial systems
      23–4
    see also financial assets purchases;
      investment

voice-dominated financial systems
  bank finance / investment relationship
    77
  cash flow / investment relationship 99,
    100
  co-ordination 12

incentive compatability 11, 12
investment
    financing 56-8, 63, 71
    levels of 101
    volatility 84, 101
liquidity 58-61
long-term financing 12
obtaining information 11-12
ready funds / investment relationship
    97, 98
ready funds volatility 72, 73

sources of funds / investment
    relationship 84, 90, 91
supply and allocation of credit 141
uses of funds 23-4
volatility
    bank finance 63, 64, 65
    internal funds 64
    investment 83-4, 101
    ready funds 72-3

weighted averaging 11

NEW DIRECTIONS IN MODERN ECONOMICS

Post-Keynesian Monetary Economics
New Approaches to Financial Modelling
Edited by Philip Arestis

Keynes's Principle of Effective Demand
Edward J. Amadeo

New Directions in Post-Keynesian Economics
Edited by John Pheby

Theory and Policy in Political Economy
Essays in Pricing, Distribution and Growth
Edited by Philip Arestis and Yiannis Kitromilides

Keynes's Third Alternative?
The Neo-Ricardian Keynesians and the Post Keynesians
Amitava Krishna Dutt and Edward J. Amadeo

Wages and Profits in the Capitalist Economy
The Impact of Monopolistic Power on Macroeconomic Performance
in the USA and UK
Andrew Henley

Prices, Profits and Financial Structures
A Post-Keynesian Approach to Competition
Gokhan Capoglu

International Perspectives on Profitability and Accumulation
Edited by Fred Moseley and Edward N. Wolff

Mr Keynes and the Post Keynesians
Principles of Macroeconomics for a Monetary Production Economy
Fernando J. Cardim de Carvalho

The Economic Surplus in Advanced Economies
Edited by John B. Davis

Foundations of Post-Keynesian Economic Analysis
Marc Lavoie

The Post-Keynesian Approach to Economics
An Alternative Analysis of Economic Theory and Policy
Philip Arestis

Income Distribution in a Corporate Economy
Russell Rimmer

The Economics of the Profit Rate
Competition, Crises and Historical Tendencies in Capitalism
Gérard Duménil and Dominique Lévy

Corporatism and Economic Performance
A Comparative Analysis of Market Economies
Andrew Henley and Euclid Tsakalotos

Competition, Technology and Money
Classical and Post-Keynesian Perspectives
Edited by Mark A. Glick

Investment Cycles in Capitalist Economies
A Kaleckian Behavioural Contribution
Jerry Courvisanos

Does Financial Deregulation Work?
A Critique of Free Market Approaches
Bruce Coggins

Pricing Theory in Post Keynesian Economics
A Realist Approach
Paul Downward

The Economics of Intangible Investment
Elizabeth Webster

Globalization and the Erosion of National Financial Systems
Is Declining Autonomy Inevitable?
Marc Schaberg

Explaining Prices in the Global Economy
A Post Keynesian Model
Henk-Jan Brinkman